THE PRESENTS OF GOD

'This book is just what we need. In this presence generation, where worship is no longer songs but a gateway into his presence, we need also to understand more about the spiritual gifts. They are, after all, his glory manifested through us. What a privilege! Starting with the word of wisdom, perhaps often left until later in most treatments of the gifts, there is encouragement on every page. This book is practical, while at the same time guiding us to the supernatural, such is the genius of Mark Stibbe's writing. We can never get too much of God's presence and we need his presents, especially to give away!'

Paul Mainwaring, Bethel Church, Redding, CA

'Mark Stibbe's book is a wonderful blend of clear biblical exposition and seasoned practical application. Mark's scholarship is evident in even a cursory reading but the impetus of this book is, "You can do this!" Highly readable and highly recommended.'

Dave Campbell, Regional Leader, Metropolitan East and West Regions,
Elim Pentecostal Church

'Mark Stibbe has done it once again – he has presented us with ancient biblical truths in a fresh, highly encouraging and compelling way. Mark has a wonderful gift for taking the mystery out of the spiritual gifts and, more importantly, the spiritual realm that God created us to experience while serving him. Mark is a true "Ephesians 4" teacher in that he not only imparts information, but also more importantly trains and equips us in learning to imitate the life that Jesus of Nazareth lived, led and empowered by the Holy Spirit. Just the simple breakdown Mark gives us of the charisma gifts into four categories – gifts of instruction, demonstration, revelation, and adoration – is so helpful. I have always especially appreciated Mark's heart in continually drawing the student of the spiritual gifts back to that truly essential fascination – a preoccupation with the gift-giver himself, Jesus!'

Marc DuPont, Mantle of Praise Ministries, Dayton, OH

'For years I've regarded Mark Stibbe as one of the most accessible theologians of our day. This book further cements that assertion. Through his amazing storytelling and practical suggestions Mark gives a fresh look at the subject of spiritual gifts. I highly recommend this book for those new to the faith and those who've been Christians for years.'

Troy Goode, Senior Pastor, New Dimension Church, Providence, RI

'Mark's relationship with his Abba explodes through these pages as he sheds new light on the gifts of the Spirit from the scriptures, current testimonies and our revival history. He writes with a father's heart as he brings the presents of God alive to us in a fresh way, thus enabling us to be the supernatural children our heavenly Father has always intended us to be.'

Hugh and Ginny Cryer, Culture Changers

THE
PRESENTS
OF
GOD

DISCOVERING YOUR SPIRITUAL GIFTS
A PRACTICAL GUIDE

MARK STIBBE

Authentic

20 19 18 17 16 15 14   7 6 5 4 3 2 1

First published 2014 by Authentic Media Limited,
52 Presley Way, Crownhill, Milton Keynes, MK8 0ES.
authenticmedia.co.uk

British Library Cataloguing in Publication Data
A catalogue record for this book is available from the British Library.

ISBN 978-1-86024-862-7   978-1-78078-252-2 (e-book)

Cover design by Paul Airy at DesignLeft (designleft.co.uk).
Printed and bound in Great Britain by CPI Group (UK) Ltd, Croydon, CR0 4YY.

DEDICATION

To my dear and loyal friend, Bill Johnson,
the most Christ-like of men.

CONTENTS

Introduction

There is nothing more precious than God's presence – it is the one thing we should all seek. This is why I am so pleased to release this brand new book on the gifts of the Holy Spirit. The gifts of the Spirit are, after all, the most telling indicators that God is among us. They are manifestations of the Holy Spirit. In other words, they are the visible signs of the Spirit's invisible presence. When miracles are performed on the streets in Jesus' name, we know God is present. When a powerful prophetic word is declared in church, we know that God is in the house.

All this shows that if we want to honour the *presence* of God, we will need to learn to honour the *presents* of God.

Think about it for a moment, whenever we receive gifts from the Holy Spirit, we welcome and enjoy the immanent and empowering presence of the King of Kings. This is because God's presence is manifested in his presents.

That is why we should always seek to practise the presence by opening our presents. Even in difficult times we can be touched by the tender hands of the Father whenever we receive a word of wisdom, feel a surge of God-given faith, speak in tongues, receive or give a prophecy.

Even when we have moved far away from him, he shows us that he is not far away from us by virtue of these manifestations of his beautiful and life-enhancing presence.

He acts through gifts such as healing.

He speaks through gifts such as wisdom.

And when he does, he proves that he is Immanuel, God with us.

In light of this, how could we ever ignore, neglect, despise or forsake such tell-tale signs of his presence?

That would be like throwing diamonds down a drain.

In this book we are looking at the spiritual gifts mentioned in 1 Corinthians 12. While I appreciate that there are other passages where spiritual gifts are mentioned, it is from this quarry that we can begin to mine the treasures of God's generosity.

Let's remind ourselves of what the Apostle Paul said about the gifts of the Spirit to the church in Corinth – a church that needed to be reminded what these gifts really were and how they were intended by God to be used:

> *Now to each one the manifestation of the Spirit is given for the common good. To one there is given through the Spirit a message of wisdom, to another a message of knowledge by means of the same Spirit, to another faith by the same Spirit, to another gifts of healing by that one Spirit, to another miraculous powers, to another prophecy, to another distinguishing between spirits, to another speaking in different kinds of tongues, and to still another the interpretation of tongues. All these are the work of one and the same Spirit, and he distributes them to each one, just as he determines.*

Nine gifts are specifically mentioned here (though there are more than these in the New Testament as a whole):

- The word of wisdom
- The word of knowledge
- The gift of faith
- Healing gifts
- The gift of miracles
- The gift of prophecy
- The gift of discernment

- The gift of speaking in tongues
- The gift of interpretation

The word of wisdom and the word of knowledge I call *gifts of instruction*. They are gifts given to teach the people of God things that cannot be learned by natural means.

The gifts of faith, healing and miracles are what I call *gifts of demonstration*. They demonstrate the power of God and the reality of God's dynamic kingdom on earth.

The gifts of prophecy and discernment I call *gifts of revelation*. They unveil the thoughts of the ascended Christ and distinguish between true and false spiritual phenomena.

The gifts of tongues and interpretation I call *gifts of adoration*. They involve a public utterance of worship in an angelic language, with an accompanying translation.

GIFTS OF INSTRUCTION
- **WORD OF WISDOM**
- **WORD OF KNOWLEDGE**

GIFTS OF DEMONSTRATION
- **FAITH**
- **HEALINGS**
- **MIRACLES**

GIFTS OF REVELATION
- **PROPHECY**
- **DISCERNMENT**

GIFTS OF ADORATION
- **TONGUES**
- **INTERPRETATION OF TONGUES**

God is a loving Father who distributes his presents throughout his family, giving to each one what they need if they are to serve him effectively. No one has all these gifts together. Together we have all the gifts.

So remember, God is the best Father in the universe, we are his adopted children, and he loves to give presents to his family. His generosity is never-ending and he calls us as his children to open our presents, to thank him for them, and then to use them to strengthen his family and to reach the world. As it says in James 1:17: '*Every good and perfect gift is from above, coming down from the Father of the heavenly lights*'. Before you start to read, please note that there are questions for you to answer in boxes throughout each chapter. These can be used either by you on your own or in a small group setting. They are designed to help you grow not only in your understanding of the gifts of the Spirit but in your use of them too. With that in mind let me encourage you to start with the following exercise.

How many of the following nine gifts of the Spirit do you think you have right now?

When you have finished the book, answer the question again!

WHICH GIFTS DO YOU HAVE?   Yes/No/Maybe

- the word of wisdom   ....
- the word of knowledge   ....
- the gift of faith   ....
- healing gifts   ....
- miraculous works   ....
- prophecy   ....
- discernment   ....
- tongues   ....
- interpretation of tongues   ....

1

THE WORD OF WISDOM

To one there is given through the Spirit a word of wisdom.

1 Corinthians 12:8

> The word of wisdom is the supernatural, God-given ability
> to say something that brings immediate clarity to a complex
> issue or a sudden resolution to a profound difficulty.

One of my favourite preachers is my good friend Bill Johnson, senior leader of Bethel Church in Redding, California – a church that has been in revival for many years.

There are many reasons why I love listening to Bill.

I love the fact that he ministers out of rest. There is no hint of striving about him. He's a man who knows that the Father loves him even before he opens his mouth. Consequently there is a complete absence of hype in his preaching style. He is cool, calm and collected!

I also love the fact that Bill's messages always lead into supernatural ministry. Bill doesn't just talk about the kingdom of God – he demonstrates it in signs, wonders and miracles. Indeed, I remember one momentous Sunday evening at St Andrew's Chorleywood when I was the senior leader there. Bill spoke about ministering healing in Jesus' name and then prayed for the sick. After he and his team finished praying he asked those who knew that they had been healed (i.e. had sensed a noticeable physical change in their medical condition) to come and stand at the front of the church and give testimony. We counted as sixty-three people shared about the miracle they'd just received. That Sunday meeting in April 2008 was the launch pad for months of Sunday night meetings in which many people were saved, healed and set free. Truly the kingdom of God is not just talk – it is power (1 Corinthians 4:20).

I love all these things about Bill's ministry but the thing I love most is the way in which he so obviously has the gift described in 1 Corinthians 12 as the word or message of wisdom, which I am defining in this chapter as 'the supernatural, God-given ability to say something that brings immediate clarity to a complex issue or a sudden resolution to a profound difficulty'.

While Bill speaks, the Holy Spirit gives him sudden insights into the secrets of the kingdom which he then utters in very brief and memorable aphorisms. Indeed, I don't know anyone who excels in this more than Bill.

Here are a few of my favourites:

If we rejoice in the acts of God without discovering his ways, we'll question who he is when he doesn't do what we've asked.

Our maturity is not evidenced by our doctrinal positions. Maturity is seen by how we treat those who differ from us.

Compromise is the door through which deception enters.

In the kingdom of God a mustard seed is bigger than a mountain, one is mightier than a thousand, and the lowest place is the highest place of all. Adjust your perception until this becomes logical.

Faith doesn't deny a problem's existence. It denies it a place of influence.

No one has ever been punished into purity.

Anyone can flatter. But true honour can only come from humility.

Fire always falls on sacrifice. Be the sacrifice.

In revival, hell is plundered and heaven is populated. Without revival, hell is populated . . . period.

One of the great tragedies in life is that historically, the Bible gets interpreted by people who are not in love . . .

This is precisely what I mean by a word of wisdom. I have seen Bill operate in this gift many times. I have watched as he smiles with surprise and delight at the fresh wisdom the Father has given him. Sometimes he'll even get down from the stage and look back up at the lectern or pulpit and say, 'That was a really good point, Bill.' That might sound big-headed to some. But it's not. It's Bill's way of helping the audience to understand that they have just been the recipients of a wisdom that comes from another world – the wisdom of heaven.

I am not alone in thinking that there's sometimes more insight in one of Bill's one-sentence asides than there is in some people's entire sermon series.

Bill is a genius at releasing words of wisdom. He is a constant reminder of the importance of the word of wisdom to the body of Christ.

As King Solomon said in Proverbs 16:16:

How much better to get wisdom than gold,
to get insight rather than silver!

Who have you heard that operates in the word of wisdom?

....

....

....

....

....

....

....

Here are seven characteristics of this priceless gift known as 'the word of wisdom'.

1. THEIR BREVITY

There are many social networks available to people who use the Internet today but one of the most popular is known as Twitter. Twitter allows a person to post a thought of no more than 140 characters at a time.

One of the useful things about this forum is that it has disciplined most people to be brief in what they say. If you can't say what you need to in a few well-phrased sentences then Twitter probably isn't for you.

When we come to words of wisdom there are two things that need to be said about them.

Firstly, words of wisdom are meant to be expressed in 'words', which is why this is called 'the word of wisdom' rather than 'the gift of wisdom'. These words of wisdom can be either written down or spoken out loud.

Secondly, words of wisdom are meant to be expressed in a few words, not in many. When we look at some of the words of wisdom given to King Solomon we can see that they were remarkable for their brevity.

Do you see someone skilled in their work? They will serve before kings; they will not serve before officials of low rank.

(Proverbs 22:29)

It is the glory of God to conceal a matter; to search out a matter is the glory of kings.

(Proverbs 25:2)

As iron sharpens iron, so one person sharpens another.

(Proverbs 27:17)

From this you can see that words of wisdom are eminently 'tweetable'. They are always expressed concisely. Indeed, the time you spend reflecting on them is comparatively far greater than the short time it takes to hear or read them.

2. THEIR MEMORABILITY

Words of wisdom are easy to remember.

It's worth noting that the book of Proverbs is really a collection of words of wisdom which the Holy Spirit gave to King Solomon and others. These words were remembered over time and then recorded in a book.

One of the reasons why these words were remembered was because words of wisdom, or Spirit-inspired proverbs, are easy to memorize. One of my favourite sayings in the book of Proverbs goes like this:

Trust in the LORD with all your heart
and lean not on your own understanding;

in all your ways submit to him,
and he will make your paths straight.

(Proverbs 3:5–6)

You can immediately see why a word of wisdom like this was easy to remember. It is concise, rhythmical and deeply personal. Even today a passage like this can be memorized quickly.

When genuine words of wisdom are uttered by an anointed communicator they become much more quickly and easily lodged in our memories than longer forms of discourse.

One of the words of wisdom I received from the Father not long ago went like this:

There are many Christians who are saved enough to go to heaven when they die. But there aren't enough Christians who are saved enough to bring heaven to earth while they live.

Another one went like this:

The treasures of discovery are found in the field of discipline.

Statements like this are memorable, both for the speaker and the listener. Their brevity and their poetry make them easy to record and recall. Genuine words of wisdom have an inbuilt memorability to them.

3. THEIR SIMPLICITY

One of the most precious aspects of the word of wisdom is that it makes complex matters very simple. When a word of wisdom is uttered or written, both the person sharing it and those who hear or read it sense the delight of something profound being made simple.

Very often when a word of wisdom is uttered, we experience the joy of two things happening simultaneously.

Firstly, we experience the joy of discovery – that we have found *'hidden treasures, riches stored in secret places'* (Isaiah 45:3). I call this the 'eureka moment'. 'Eureka!' comes from the classical Greek word meaning 'I've discovered it!', 'it' referring to some vital information or insight.

It's what Archimedes, the ancient Greek mathematician, allegedly exclaimed when he slipped into his bath and realized that the volume of the water that he had just displaced must be in direct proportion to the volume of the part of his body that had just been submerged.

In the utterance of every genuine word of wisdom, we experience a 'eureka moment'. We sense that something obscure has been made clear, something concealed has been revealed, something hard has been made simple.

Secondly, we experience the joy of something beautifully expressed. A word of wisdom is truth expressed in an extremely satisfying way. There is a heavenly beauty about the language. Often it can be almost lyrical or poetic. Indeed, the utterance of a true word of wisdom can often cause an audible 'Yes!' in the audience.

Another of my favourite sayings from the book of Proverbs goes like this in the New King James Version:

> *A word fitly spoken is like apples of gold in settings of silver.*
>
> (Proverbs 25:11, NKJV)

A word of wisdom therefore takes us on a journey from mystery to clarity and does so in a way that is beautiful, not just truthful.

4. THEIR ADAPTABILITY

Words of wisdom are wonderfully adaptable both in relation to content and context. In relation to content, the wisdom you receive can be about any matter, great and small.

Some words of wisdom are about the Father's plan for human history – a plan that focuses on Jesus Christ, who is the Wisdom of God, and on the central event of his life, his atoning death on the cross.

The Bible makes it very clear that it takes supernatural insight to understand how the crucifixion of a carpenter outside Jerusalem is the climax of history – how the cross is the key to unlocking everything.

Some words of wisdom are accordingly about large matters – the secret wisdom about God's cosmic plans. Others may be about smaller issues – like how to resolve an issue in a local church.

With regard to context, words of wisdom are as gloriously adaptable as they are with regard to content.

You can just as easily receive a word of wisdom in the boardroom of a non-Christian business as you can in the vestry of a Christian church.

Remember Daniel? He used the heavenly wisdom which the Father gave him in the governmental sphere. He used spiritual revelation to bring spiritual solutions to political problems.

Always value the adaptability of wisdom.

Keep in mind that you're a child of the King. You belong to another realm – the realm of heaven. You therefore have privileged recourse to a secret wisdom that the world can't access. You can reach for supernatural solutions to practical problems. You can pull down heaven's ideas about earth's issues! This is because you are not a human citizen having heavenly experiences. You are a heavenly citizen having human experiences!

5. THEIR CONSISTENCY

A genuine word of wisdom will have an inherent consistency to it. It will be consistent in relation to two things.

Firstly, it will be consistent with the written Word, that is, the Bible.

No authentic utterance of wisdom will ever be inconsistent with what the Bible teaches. A word of wisdom is spoken revelation, but *spoken* revelation – if it's authentic – always accords with the *written* revelation of God's Word.

Every word of wisdom must be weighed and tested against the written Word of God. If it doesn't agree with what the Bible plainly teaches it should immediately be rejected.

Secondly, a word of wisdom will also be consistent with the *Incarnate Word* – the Word made flesh, that is, Jesus Christ.

When a genuine word of wisdom is uttered, it's going to sound like Jesus. The listener will often think, 'That's the kind of thing that Jesus would say.'

So, if it doesn't sound like him, ignore it.

If it sounds like him, receive it.

This brings me to an important point. While words of wisdom have less authority than Scripture, especially the words of Jesus, we should never underestimate the authority which true words of wisdom carry.

We are the adopted children of the High King of Heaven. When he shares the secrets of his kingdom with us, those secrets – once spoken – carry authority.

Business men and women in the boardroom will sense it. Teachers in the staff room will sense it. Officers in a military headquarters will sense it.

If we utter a word of wisdom that comes from the Father-heart of God, its authority will be recognized even when its author is not.

Words of wisdom that are consistent with the Bible and with Jesus have spiritual authority.

6. THEIR SPONTANEITY

A word of wisdom is something that comes to a person suddenly. It is not something that you come up with over time. It comes unexpectedly – in a way that delights and surprises you. In other words, words of wisdom do not come to us gradually and in our natural minds. They come quickly and to our spiritual minds. As with all the gifts, we need to remember that the word of wisdom is a gift of the Holy Spirit. Receiving a word of wisdom accordingly comes suddenly, supernaturally and sovereignly. It comes when the Holy Spirit decides and as the Holy Spirit determines.

It does not come as a result of academic learning or natural erudition. It comes as a result of the Father deciding to give us a gift we don't deserve – a grace gift from heaven.

When I have uttered words of wisdom in the past, it has often been in the context of teaching God's Word. It seems that when I'm opening the Scriptures and declaring what my Father is showing me that I am more open to the Holy Spirit than just about any other time.

Consequently, I sometimes have a sudden experience of receiving and sharing an insight that I've not had before, or I've not had in that form before.

Words of wisdom come spontaneously. They are like gold dust from heaven; you have to catch them before they disappear.

7. THEIR PRODUCTIVITY

Genuine words of wisdom will always be productive. They will bear spiritual fruit in the lives of those who are prepared to say 'yes' to them. In Isaiah 55:9–11, we read this:

As the heavens are higher than the earth, so are my ways higher than your ways and my thoughts than your thoughts. As the rain and the snow come down from heaven, and do not return to it without watering the earth and making it bud and flourish, so that it yields seed for the sower and bread for the eater, so is my word that goes out from my mouth: it will not return to me empty, but will accomplish what I desire and achieve the purpose for which I sent it.

Whatever the Father says, and however he says it, it's going to be productive. It's going to accomplish what he desires and it's going to fulfil the purpose for which it is sent.

This is true for authentic words of wisdom as well. Heavenly wisdom is productive. As it says in the book of James:

The wisdom that comes from heaven is first of all pure; then peace-loving, considerate, submissive, full of mercy and good fruit, impartial and sincere.

(James 3:17)

Notice the words 'peace-loving'. I remember a British Army officer who served in the Falklands War sharing a testimony of how he and his men were hopelessly outnumbered, pinned down by the enemy and in danger of suffering many casualties. He was a Christian, so he took a moment on his own and prayed for wisdom. The Father gave him the solution: 'Even though you're outnumbered, in order to avoid a senseless waste of life, ask the enemy to surrender and promise honourable terms.' He did just that and the senior officer of the opposing force told his soldiers to lay down their arms and surrender to the far smaller British unit.

Truly words of wisdom are peace-loving. They are always productive; they bear fruit in extraordinary ways.

THE BEAUTY OF WORDS OF WISDOM CONSISTS IN THEIR

- Brevity
- Memorability
- Simplicity
- Adaptability
- Consistency
- Spontaneity
- Productivity

I hope at this point you're persuaded that the word of wisdom is a vital spiritual gift. In case you still need to be convinced, here are two more reasons why I believe that we need this gift right now.

The first is because there is a rising tide of persecution of Christians throughout the world. Indeed, there's evidence of an increase in persecution in the western world, including in the UK. If this is true then the word of wisdom is going to be an indispensable spiritual gift for many believers. More and more of us are going to be asked tough questions in intimidating situations, especially because of our faith in Jesus and all that this entails. In those contexts we will need words of wisdom rather than the wisdom of words if we are to answer our accusers in a compelling way.

In light of this it is heartening to know that Jesus promised we would receive such wisdom under pressure, and Jesus never lies. His promises are forever true and he never fails to fulfil them. Jesus tells his disciples that when they are brought before legal and political authorities, '*I will give you words and wisdom that none of your adversaries will be able to resist or contradict*' (Luke 21:15).

How we need to ask our heavenly Father for more wisdom in our lives, especially more words of wisdom.

That's the first reason – and it's a good reason.

The second reason is because the church today needs to be a church of both truth and experience together, not one to the neglect of the other. We will not transform let alone reform our culture with experience alone. We need to be truth-tellers and wisdom-bringers too.

I believe the world is not just waiting for a church that's filled with power. It's also waiting for a church that's filled with wisdom.

Jesus Christ is both the power and the wisdom of God (1 Corinthians 1:24).

If we as a church are to reflect Jesus in an integrated and convincing way, then we will need to bring about a remarriage of power and wisdom. We will need to be a people who move in the supernatural power of God in a manifest and very real way. We will also need to be a people who receive and transmit words of heavenly wisdom in a humble and life-changing way.

> **Are you a person of both power and wisdom? Which of these do you need to work on right now?**
>
> ....
> ....
> ....
> ....
> ....
> ....

As I conclude this chapter I want to leave you with some practical thoughts on how to grow in the gift known as 'the word of wisdom'.

Firstly, simply ask your heavenly Father for this gift. In James 1:5 we read:

> *If any of you lacks wisdom, you should ask God, who gives generously to all without finding fault, and it will be given to you.*

We have a very generous Father who loves to give gifts to us, whether we deserve them or not. If the word of wisdom is a gift you really long for, then ask Abba Father for it and trust that he will answer your prayer.

Watch for instances in your life from now on where you have sudden insights and solutions to complex matters and situations. Every time you realize that you're growing in this grace, be grateful.

The more gratitude you express, the more grace will be released to you.

Secondly, get as close as you can to people who have the gift and who regularly operate in the 'word of wisdom'. One of the great benefits of the recent technological revolution is that it has created a global network of information that we can quickly access. This means that I can listen to a sermon tonight that was preached in America this morning. I don't have to travel all the way to the States to hear it. I can simply download a podcast from a church's website.

One way to grow in the word of wisdom is to listen regularly to those anointed communicators who have this gift. That way you can begin to swim in the wake of their gifting. This is not so that you end up sounding like them. No one wants you to be a clone of some other preacher. It's because this kind of thing is more often caught than taught. So expose your heart to other people who clearly have this gift.

Finally, learn to live consistently in the reality of the kingdom of heaven. I believe that the word of wisdom is given to those who see the kingdom of God coming into their midst on a regular basis. In other words, the wisdom of heaven is given to those who live in the atmosphere of heaven.

Let me share a testimony which illustrates exactly what I mean. Not long ago my good friend Marc Dupont shared this story:

We heard a great testimony tonight in Sheffield, England. Maureen, who was in a meeting I did several years ago here, responded to a word about long-term stomach disorders while in that meeting. Within three days she was set free after suffering for more than twenty-five years with constant stomach problems and pain which also affected her back. Her doctors had previously taken her off all meds because nothing seemed to help her condition.

Marc then added this:

> When the kingdom of God is moving on earth, the realm of the always possible is invading the realm of the often impossible.

That's a word of wisdom! It's a brief utterance in which the secrets of the kingdom of heaven are made accessible to all in a memorable way.

But notice this: that word of wisdom followed on from a demonstration and manifestation of the kingdom of heaven.

And here's my point: those who most often live in the atmosphere of heaven are those who are most likely to access the wisdom of heaven.

If you think about it, this makes perfect sense. You have to live in the realm of heaven if you're going to speak the language of heaven.

To what extent do you live consistently in the atmosphere, the reality and the manifest presence of the kingdom of heaven?

....

....

....

....

....

....

A FINAL THOUGHT . . .

I began this chapter celebrating my friend Bill Johnson and his supernatural, God-given ability to utter words that bring immediate clarity to complex issues. I want to end with another one of his words of wisdom.

Let me set this in context. Sometimes a word is uttered that sounds wise but on subsequent reflection turns out to be less insightful than you first thought. A case in point is a statement that has often been uttered in circles that I have moved in, particularly at Christian conferences. The statement goes something like this: 'It is more important to seek God's face than his hand – more important to seek the Giver than the gifts.'

I remember when I first heard this I thought that it sounded good. But then I started writing this book, *The Presents of God* – a book whose primary purpose is to help the reader seek and find their God-given gifts. That got me thinking about whether it's wrong to ask the Father to release good gifts – whether it's actually wrong to seek his hand. Surely that's what Jesus encouraged us to do anyway!

I have accordingly become less convinced about the credibility of this apparent word of wisdom. Then I heard this word of wisdom from Bill Johnson – a word that forms a fitting and hopeful place to end this chapter:

> No one was ever discouraged, corrected, or criticized by Jesus for seeking his gifts. 'Seek the giver, not the gift' is a religious idea that comes from people who fear excess more than they fear lack. If you happen to find 'his hand' instead of 'his face', just look up. They're not that far apart.

What am I going to do as a result of what I've learned in this chapter?

··

··

··

··

··

··

··

··

··

··

··

··

··

··

2

THE WORD OF KNOWLEDGE

To another is given the word of knowledge by the same Spirit.

1 Corinthians 12:9

The word of knowledge is the God-given ability to express knowledge which has not been gained through human learning but rather through the Holy Spirit.

I want to share with you what I experienced one time when I spoke at a Sunday evening meeting in a London church; it taught me a lot about the word of knowledge.

Just before I was due to preach, the congregation engaged in about an hour of sung worship. It was passionate praise and the presence of God became very real to most, if not all, of those gathered where we were meeting. We should not be surprised at this. Remember that the Bible never said God *inhibits* the praises of his people. It says he *inhabits* the praises of his people. When we praise him with all our heart, mind, soul and strength, he makes his presence felt. He can't resist it!

Just after the singing had died down, one of the leaders stood up and began to share about a conference he'd attended the previous day in Wales. He shared how the Father had given his wife a message about the relationship between humility and authority which had proved to be extremely anointed.

At that moment something began to happen in my heart. I had prepared a message to deliver but as those two words 'humility' and 'authority' were mentioned, the Holy Spirit started to show me truths I hadn't seen or heard before about the relationship between these two thoughts. As I stood up to speak I realized that the message I had planned to bring wasn't the message of the moment. I ditched my notes and proceeded to trust my heavenly Father to give me whatever revelation he wanted me to impart.

Trusting in God rather than leaning on my own understanding, supernatural knowledge began to flow into and then through me – not just a few insights but many, one after another, in an unbroken chain of revelation for more than forty-five minutes. I knew that I knew things that I hadn't learned from books but from the Holy Spirit. I knew that I knew things that were supernatural rather than natural in origin and I also knew that I was being given the words, the vocabulary and even the poetry with which to express them.

All through the talk I could tell by people's reactions that the Holy Spirit was imparting knowledge and that this was his message not mine. And when it came to the response, a large percentage of the congregation came to the front to kneel at the cross and press in for that increased humility which releases increased authority.

Have you ever heard a talk in which you sensed the speaker was receiving and sharing knowledge that was inspired by the Holy Spirit? ....

....

....

....

....

If ever I experienced what it's like to utter a message of knowledge, it was on that memorable Sunday night in London.

I have started this chapter with a personal testimony because I believe that it reaches to the very heart of what Paul meant when he talked about the spiritual gift called 'the word' or 'the message' of 'knowledge'.

The word or message of knowledge is essentially a gift in which God imparts spiritual knowledge to someone who then speaks it out to others in words anointed by the Spirit. This kind of knowledge is knowledge about the infinite vistas of the grace of God made available to us through the cross of Christ and made real to us through the Holy Spirit. The word of knowledge is therefore the articulation of a revelation – a revelation that comes from the deep and endless recesses of the Father heart of God. It is an anointed celebration and vocalization of the amazing inheritance that is ours in Christ.

Have you ever received and shared insights that you knew you hadn't learned but were given by the Holy Spirit?

....

....

....

....

....

....

Before I describe this gift in more detail I want to issue a plea concerning knowledge in general.

When I speak of the word of knowledge as knowledge gained by revelation I am not for one moment suggesting that we neglect knowledge that is gained through education. Having studied Literature and

Theology to the level of a doctorate I fully appreciate the supreme value of knowledge that we can accumulate through listening to people with brilliant minds and poring over books with lasting insights.

Human study and learning is not to be despised. In fact, I would argue that the spiritual discipline of study is one that urgently needs to be rediscovered today, especially in those Christian circles where the heart is emphasized but the mind is neglected. Studying the Word of God in depth – or other subjects that are generally taught by schools and universities – is not necessarily hostile to authentic Christian spirituality or unproductive in the kingdom of God. Actually, as the lives of people like C.S. Lewis conclusively demonstrate, study can enrich the soul and advance the Kingdom immeasurably.

In this respect C.S. Lewis was surely right when he encouraged all believers to cultivate a discipleship of the heart and the mind. We desperately need light in our heads not just heat in our hearts if we are to be a people on fire. We urgently need to rediscover the fullness of the Great Commandment in Mark 12, where Jesus calls us to love the Father not only with our hearts (emotionally), our souls (spiritually) and our strength (physically) but also with our minds (intellectually).

Engaging with God intellectually and theologically is not a demonic or a dangerous enterprise. It is an adventure that all believers are meant to cultivate. In fact G.K. Chesterton said that theology is essentially worshipping God with our minds. It is a form of adoration.

And if you think about it, that has to be true. How can we fall in love with someone and not think deeply, frequently and intensely about them? How can we adore Jesus without reflecting on the height, breadth and depth of his infinite affections? Thoughtless adoration is a contradiction in terms.

Theology – and indeed other academic disciplines too – is accordingly of great value and vital for a fully-orbed and integrated discipleship. It is as important as the brain is to the body. It is as vital as thinking is to living.

No one should despise naturally acquired knowledge. A good education can be the fertile soil in which revelation thrives.

To those who love the living water of the Holy Spirit, I say this: give as much emphasis to thinking as to drinking.

> **To what extent do you value knowledge gained by human study – especially knowledge of the Bible?**
>
> ....
>
> ....
>
> ....
>
> ....
>
> ....
>
> ....

At the same time, I know this: that studying the things of God – and indeed the broad issues of life itself – can sometimes be lifeless and very unrewarding.

I have, on many occasions, listened to highly intelligent scholars whose lectures and writing are at best dull and dry and at worst cynical and destructive.

Conversely, I have often heard Spirit-filled Christians who have no academic credentials whatsoever utter truths which have more spiritual light in a passing phrase than others without the Spirit have in an entire book.

Why is this? It is because the mind of man without the Spirit of God is a very vulnerable organ. Indeed, the natural mind without the Holy Spirit can never unearth the kind of spiritual knowledge which is found by the mind saturated and directed by the Holy Spirit of God.

The mind enlightened by God's Spirit, on the other hand, has unique access to spiritual insights. That is precisely why we need spiritual not natural minds to discover the timeless treasures of God's truth. No one will ever reach up to heaven and bring spiritual knowledge to earth with the natural mind alone. We need Spirit-baptized minds and faith-filled hearts to do that.

> **How good are you at filtering the good from the bad when you're listening to or reading the views of educated people?**
>
> ....
> ....
> ....
> ....
> ....
> ....

With all that in mind, let's now look at the word of knowledge more closely.

The most important thing to remember right at the start is that the word of knowledge is not something that I can earn. It is something I receive.

Remember: the word of knowledge is a spiritual gift. It is one of the Father's presents. The word of knowledge is therefore not the expression of natural or human knowledge. Rather, it is the articulation of knowledge that is given by the supernatural operation of the Holy Spirit. It is Spirit-inspired knowledge uttered in Spirit-anointed words. It's the kind of knowledge that I was given 'in the moment', as it were, on that Sunday night as I preached. It is the kind of knowledge that comes to you on the wings of a welcome and unexpected visitation.

Let me underscore this by stressing a number of important things about the word of knowledge. I am going to do this using the words 'How' ('How does this gift come to us?'), 'Who' ('Who receives this gift?'), 'What' ('What kind of knowledge is given?'), and 'Why' ('Why is this gift important?').

How?

The word of knowledge is the second of the nine spiritual gifts which Paul mentions in 1 Corinthians 12:8–11. When considering how this gift comes to us, we should remember how the other eight gifts in the list come to a believer. Here's the list again:

GIFTS OF INSRUCTION
- **WORD OF WISDOM**
- **WORD OF KNOWLEDGE**

GIFTS OF DEMONSTRATION
- **FAITH**
- **HEALINGS**
- **MIRACLES**

GIFTS OF REVELATION
- **PROPHECY**
- **DISCERNMENT**

GIFTS OF ADORATION
- **TONGUES**
- **INTERPRETATION OF TONGUES**

Notice something important about the other eight gifts. All of them come spontaneously to the person receiving them. They come in the moment, as it were. They are given suddenly, sometimes unexpectedly.

The word of wisdom is something that you receive spontaneously. The one receiving the gift is as surprised and delighted as the ones listening that heavenly wisdom has suddenly been communicated.

The gift of faith is a gift that comes spontaneously. You have a challenge in front of you and you experience an unanticipated but welcome surge of unshakeable confidence that your heavenly Father is about to move in power to remove it. This kind of special faith is received spontaneously.

The gifts of healing are spontaneous too. Confronted by a situation of sickness, the Holy Spirit suddenly enables and empowers you to lay hands on the sick and pray for their healing or to issue a word of command and see that infirmity healed.

The gift of miraculous works is also spontaneous. In a situation where it seems humanly impossible to get a breakthrough, the Spirit of God anoints you to deliver the oppressed, to raise the dead, to still storms, to multiply food, and so on. All these things happen spontaneously.

The gift of prophecy is a gift that comes spontaneously too. Revelation comes to you suddenly, allowing you to know the mind of Christ about a person or a situation.

The gift of discernment is also a gift that comes spontaneously. As you look at a person or a predicament, the Father suddenly gives you the special ability to evaluate whether these things are motivated by the flesh, by the devil or by the Holy Spirit of God.

The gift of tongues is a gift that comes spontaneously. One moment you are speaking to the Father in your normal, native tongue. The next you are overflowing with adoration in a language not your own – the love language of the angels in heaven.

The gift of interpretation is a gift that comes spontaneously. As you listen to someone expressing their worship in a language which is not their own, the Holy Spirit suddenly gives you a translation of those angelic words into your own language, which you then offer to the congregation.

The eight gifts I've just mentioned are gifts that come spontaneously or suddenly. If this is true of the other gifts, it must also be true of the word of knowledge. When the word of knowledge comes to us it comes spontaneously. One moment you don't have this knowledge; the next moment you do. One moment you're not speaking about it; the next moment you are.

WHO?

Who receives the word of knowledge? The simple answer is that any believer can receive the word of knowledge. It is the Holy Spirit who determines and decides who receives which gift and when. As the Dove of Heaven, he can alight on any shoulder at any time.

Having said that, I do believe there are certain people who are more strategically positioned to receive this gift than others. Given that the word of knowledge is what I'm calling 'a gift of instruction', it seems logical that someone who is anointed to teach will be likely to receive this gift. Indeed, I don't see how anyone who is called to be an anointed communicator can do without the word of wisdom and the word of knowledge in their spiritual utility belts. The person called to teach is a person called to communicate fresh insights into old truths. They are called to bring out treasures old and new.

One of my favourite verses in the Bible is all about the call to teach. It's Matthew 13:52. In *The Message* version of the Bible, this is what Jesus says:

Every student well-trained in God's kingdom is like the owner of a general store who can put his hands on anything you need, old or new, exactly when you need it.

Those who are called to teach God's truth are like a householder who goes into his secret storeroom and draws out treasures that are old and new. The original Greek text describes this treasure using the word *thesaurus*. Teachers are people who find new words to articulate old truths.

If this is true, then what happens when a word of knowledge is given that is actually more complex, mysterious and glorious than we realize?

When we receive a word of knowledge, we are going into two treasure rooms at the same time. We are going into the treasure room of heaven and bringing out gems that we haven't seen or heard before. At the same time we are going into the treasure room of our own heart and drawing out the gems that we have seen and heard in our own studies. When we give a message or a word of knowledge, we are expressing insights that are both brand new to us and at the same time old and familiar. Things that we haven't seen before are combined with things that we have. A fusion takes place between that which is received from heaven and that which is learned on earth.

I therefore propose that the word of knowledge is likely to be given to those who are called to communicate God's truth. It is likely to be given to those who are prepared to break away from what they have prepared and go with what the Father is saying in the moment. It is given to those who keep storing up heavenly treasure in their hearts – the treasures of God's timeless Word – and who are always open to the Holy Spirit.

If you're a preacher, ask the Father for this gift.

WHAT?

What do we come to know when this gift is given to us? What is the content of the knowledge given to us supernaturally?

I appreciate that I'm being controversial here but I want to propose there has been a great deal of confusion in recent decades about the word of knowledge. Too many preachers have wrongly taught that the word of knowledge is a supernatural insight into another person's heart which is then spoken to them, giving them a sudden realization that God is real and God is present. In their understanding, the word of knowledge involves suddenly knowing something about someone else that only God could have told you.

I don't believe that this is what Paul meant by the word of knowledge. I would argue that this is the gift of prophecy. That's why in 1 Corinthians 14 Paul talks about what happens to unbelievers when they come into a meeting where believers are giving prophetic words. Some of these prophetic words will be about the unbelievers themselves. When they hear the secrets of their hearts exposed, Paul says that *'they will fall down and worship God, exclaiming, "God is really among you!"'*

So let me say as lovingly as possible that we need to learn to distinguish between the message of knowledge and the gift of prophecy. The two are not to be confused. I'll try and put it simply.

When the gift of prophecy is given, we come to know things about *other people* that we couldn't have known before.

When the word of knowledge is given, we come to know things about *God* we couldn't have known before.

While both gifts involve receiving divine revelation, the purpose of the two is very different.

Have you been influenced by the view that a word of knowledge is a supernatural insight into someone else's heart?

....

....

....

....

....

....

Perhaps the key passage for understanding the word of knowledge is something that Paul says earlier in the same letter in which he writes about the spiritual gifts. As you read 1 Corinthians 2:10–12, please note how Paul is talking about 'knowledge' here, as can be seen by his use of the verb 'know':

> *The Spirit searches all things, even the deep things of God. For who **knows** a person's thoughts except their own spirit within them? In the same way no one **knows** the thoughts of God except the Spirit of God. What we have received is not the spirit of the world, but the Spirit who is from God, so that we may understand what God has freely given us.*

From this we can infer three important things about the gift known as the word of knowledge.

1. This gift enables us to know the thoughts of God

It gives us access to what the Father is thinking, to what the Father knows. The knowledge expressed in the word of knowledge is therefore knowledge about the Father's mind and the Father's heart. Those who utter genuine words of knowledge tell us the Father's thoughts.

2. This knowledge is given so that we have a better grasp of grace

As Paul puts it, it is given 'so that we may understand what God has freely given us'. Those who have the authentic word of knowledge are accordingly relentless celebrators of grace. They dive deeper than others into the ocean of the Father's extravagant love and give voice to what they find there.

3. The Holy Spirit alone knows the thoughts in the heart of our heavenly Father

Accordingly, this knowledge can only come from the Holy Spirit and can only come to those who have received the Holy Spirit. Those who operate with the natural mind alone cannot access this knowledge. Their minds need to be baptized in the Holy Spirit if they are ever to access this heavenly knowledge.

The good news is that Paul teaches that we have received the Spirit that is from God. When we put our faith in Jesus, we are filled with the Spirit. This means that we can know what the Father is thinking through the Spirit of God who is not only living within us but at the same time searching the secret places in the Father's heart.

WHY?

Why do we need the 'word of knowledge'?

Like all the gifts of the Spirit, the word of knowledge is given for the common good. In other words, the word of knowledge is not meant to be a private revelation which only blesses the person receiving it. It is meant to be shared with the Body of Christ, the church, so that everyone can be strengthened in their faith and enlightened in their understanding.

Perhaps it's worth stressing here that this particular gift is not referred to by Paul as 'the *gift* of knowledge' but 'the *word* of knowledge.' When this knowledge is given by the Holy Spirit, it is meant to be communicated with other believers.

Look at what Paul adds in 1 Corinthians 2:13, when he's talking about the knowledge given to us by the Holy Spirit:

This is what we speak, not in words taught us by human wisdom but in words taught by the Spirit, explaining spiritual realities with Spirit-taught words.

When it comes to the word of knowledge, we speak out what we are given. Words of knowledge are therefore not secrets that are meant to be kept to the one receiving them, as badges of some kind of higher spirituality. They are insights that are meant to be spoken out so that everyone in the church may be blessed.

Words of knowledge need to be spoken out and sometimes they even need to be sung. Indeed, I believe that some of our most inspiring worship songs start off as words of knowledge. These insights stretch the resources of prose to the point where poetry and song begin. Songs like 'Here is Love', which was first sung spontaneously in the Spirit in the 1904 Welsh revival, started out – I believe – as words of knowledge.

Here is love, vast as the ocean,
Loving-kindness as the flood,
When the Prince of Life, our Ransom,
Shed for us his precious blood.
Who his love will not remember?
Who can cease to sing his praise?
He can never be forgotten,
Throughout heav'n's eternal days.
William Rees (1802–1883), Public Domain

I can think of other examples, too, including in my own life. For instance, I remember one occasion when God helped me to know one simple truth: 'One touch from the king changes everything.' I then started uttering that phrase in many sermons all over the world before exploring it in more depth in *One Touch from the King* (Authentic, 2007). To date I know of at least three popular worship songs which have been inspired by what was effectively a word of knowledge.

So there are without doubt times when we suddenly know the rich and royal truths of heaven and we can't help expressing them in lyrical songs of love.

> **Can you think of any other songs that might have been inspired by a word of knowledge?**
>
> ....
> ....
> ....
> ....
> ....
> ....

All this talk of love brings me to one final thought, and this has to do with the difference between the word of wisdom and the word of knowledge.

Clearly these two gifts overlap in some measure. They are both gifts of instruction and the dividing line between wisdom and knowledge is often more fluid than fixed. At the same time, my definitions of these two gifts do suggest a difference in the content of what is received.

Here they are once again:

- **The word of wisdom** is . . . the supernatural, God-given ability to say something that brings immediate clarity to a complex issue or a sudden resolution to a profound difficulty.
- **The word of knowledge** is . . . the God-given ability to express knowledge which has not been gained through human learning but rather through the Holy Spirit.

Seen this way, there are clearly differences as well as similarities when it comes to the content of revelation in both gifts. There are also differences in the contexts in which both these gifts tend to thrive.

The word of wisdom thrives in a specific context. The same is true of the word of knowledge.

Let me try and express this as clearly and succinctly as I can in a statement which I believe to be true often enough to constitute a truism:

> While the word of wisdom comes to those who see constant demonstrations of God's power, the word of knowledge comes to those who are intimately acquainted with God's love.

I appreciate that this may be a little demanding so let's backtrack together for a moment. In order to understand this truism, please remember what I wrote in the last chapter about the word of wisdom. I said there that to speak the wisdom of heaven you have to spend time in the atmosphere of heaven. The word of wisdom therefore comes to those who frequently see God's power at work – to those who see the kingdom of heaven invading earth on a consistent basis. It seems accordingly that there is an inextricable link between the power of God and the wisdom of God. Indeed, Paul connects these two words decisively when he talks about Jesus Christ as both the power and the wisdom of God in 1 Corinthians 1. The more power you witness, the more wisdom you access.

With the word of knowledge, the context is different. While the word of wisdom comes to those who frequently see God's power, the word of knowledge comes to those who consistently know what it is to experience the affectionate love of God. Put another way, the insights that belong to our Father in heaven are given to those who value intimacy with the Father here on earth.

Perhaps all this will become a little clearer if we consider how 'knowledge' is understood in the Bible. Many of us reading this book will probably have an understanding of knowledge which has its origins in ancient Greek culture. So much of western civilization has been influenced by the thinking of classical Greece – by the minds of Aristotle, Plato and many others. The Bible, however, doesn't really come out of this western background. It comes from the East, in fact from the Middle East.

Now all this has radical implications for the word 'knowledge' and indeed 'the word of knowledge'. In the Middle East, knowledge is not primarily intellectual, as it is in the West. It is relational. Knowing is not primarily propositional; it is personal. If I show you a photograph of my beloved, adoptive father and indeed I tell you about him, you will have a propositional knowledge of him. You will know about him cognitively. I, however, knew him personally.

There is accordingly a world of difference between the Greek and the Hebrew way of knowing. To the Greeks – as for many of us – knowledge is intellectual, theoretical and cerebral. To the Hebrews, knowing is relational, personal and experiential.

That is why I want to propose that those who operate in the word of knowledge are those who cultivate a lifestyle of intimacy with God. If power is the environment in which words of wisdom are given, love is the environment in which words of knowledge are given. Put another way, the greater the intimacy, the greater the insights.

So let me encourage you to tuck yourself under the arms of your heavenly Father, lean on his chest, and turn one ear to his face. That way you will position yourself to hear the whispering voice from his mouth and the gentle beating of his heart. That way you will be ready to hear and share his words of knowledge.

No one ever excelled in the word of knowledge who wasn't first a lover of God.

And how we need this gift in the church today!

As the prophet Hosea once said, God's people are destroyed for lack of knowledge (Hosea 4:6). We need a fresh emphasis on the knowledge of the Word and on the word of knowledge.

Perhaps it's time to heed the words of that great God-lover and songwriter, King David: '*Be still, and* know *that I am God.*'

What am I going to do as a result of what I've learned in this chapter?

....

....

....

....

....

....

....

....

....

....

....

....

....

3

THE GIFT OF FAITH

To another faith by the same Spirit.

1 Corinthians 12:9

> The gift of faith is the supernatural capacity to believe that
> God is about to move in a very special way to reveal his glory.

I wonder if you've ever had the experience of knowing with an unshakeable certainty that God was about to do something extraordinary – something that would, in the normal course of events, seem impossible. It didn't matter how sceptical others were or how tired you were, you just knew with complete assurance that someone was about to get saved or healed, that some great difficulty was about to be supernaturally resolved, some big need was going to be met. You just knew that a breakthrough was coming.

I have had moments like this in my life.

Three decades ago I was a youth pastor. I remember planning a youth meeting for the following Sunday night. The theme was what Jesus has done for us at Calvary. Three days before the meeting I had a sudden and unexpected surge of confidence that young people were going to have a life-changing encounter with Jesus that Sunday. I spoke it out to my fellow youth leaders. The following Sunday evening twelve teenagers gave their lives to Christ at the end of the talk.

I remember another time when I needed £3,000 for the ministry I was leading. This was simply to survive the summer financially. One Tuesday morning I felt led to thank God as if the money had already arrived. I went in to work a few hours later and there was a cheque on my desk for £2,997. A church I had never visited had decided to take up an offering for the ministry the week before. Again, faith had been rewarded.

Not long ago I was asked to go to a church and speak on a Sunday morning about God's power to heal the sick. As I prepared my talk I had that same rush of supernatural confidence that people were going to be healed in the meetings. Sure enough, as I mentioned medical conditions that the Holy Spirit was highlighting to me, people began to stand all over the auditorium. Several started waving their arms and cheering, signalling that they had felt healed just in the act of standing. Some wrote afterwards to tell me what had happened. One shared the following testimony:

Around three years ago I had what would be best described as a cold, and being a typical bloke did nothing about it. This then turned into a cough and within a couple of weeks turned into full-blown pleurisy. I was hospitalized and later released with some tablets and the normal 'not much more we can do'.

Over the next 12 months I started getting more bouts of pleurisy and this then turned into the start of angina and pericarditis, when the sac around my heart became infected. I was put on painkillers, statins, etc.

In December 2009 I was rushed into hospital with a suspected heart attack, this turned out to be a full angina attack and I was released.

Since December 2009 I have been under regular doctor's health checks, and the diagnosis has not changed. Not a lot could be done other than managing the pain with painkillers.

I have lived a normal life since and not worried about the pain or the coughing . . . it has just been there for me to live with. God has blessed me in so many ways since then. Although I have seen people healed I have never believed myself to be worthy of this. At times the worldly side of me has arisen and I have been cynical about the whole thing.

Then at my church there was a teaching given on healing. At the end of the teaching you started praying for people with head injuries and then people with chest problems. I surrendered myself to this prayer and waited. I invited the Holy Spirit to come and heal me and surrendered myself to this whilst you were praying. I immediately felt as though a crack rushed around my chest and I sensed a release of all pain. My chest felt as though it was free. It was as if a clay urn had been around my chest, restricting my day-to-day life, and the Holy Spirit had broken this into a thousand pieces and I was able to breathe. It was immediate.

Now, 48 hours later . . . I am in no pain, can breathe freely and feel well. My wife has seen an immediate change in me physically and mentally.

So does healing work? Oh yes, it does. Through the grace and love of God's Holy Spirit I am healed!

Have you ever had this experience of being unshakeably certain that God was about to do something extraordinary – and you saw it happen?

....

....

....

....

....

....

What is this 'surge of supernatural confidence' which we see in these testimonies? It is what the Bible calls 'the gift of faith'.

The gift of faith is a gift of grace, like all the spiritual gifts. This means that it is not something you can earn or something you can work up in your own strength. Rather, it is something freely given by your heavenly Father and something which you receive as his beloved child.

From time to time you may experience moments when you know with a complete certainty that God is about to do something mighty. That is a gift – and specifically it is the gift of faith.

What then do we mean by faith?

Faith is essentially being certain about something that you don't yet see with your natural, physical eyes.

I don't yet see Jesus but he is alive, raised by his Father from the dead. The Bible says that he once was dead but now is alive for evermore. Even though he's invisible to my eyes, I now exercise faith and believe that Jesus is alive, that he's real and that I can have an eternal friendship with him, beginning right now.

Faith in this case is being sure about someone you don't yet see with your eyes. And the reward of faith is one day seeing with your eyes what you have believed. One day I'm going to see Jesus. One day, Jesus is going to come back in great glory and I will see him face to face. I'm going to see the one in whom I've put my trust. I'm sure of that.

Faith is therefore vital for the Christian life – as vital as oxygen is to normal life. Every Christian is called to be faithful or full of faith. She or he is called to trust in the invisible and believe the impossible.

> **How strong is your faith in the person of Jesus right now?**
>
> ....
>
> ....
>
> ....
>
> ....
>
> ....
>
> ....
>
> ....

We can go even further than this, however. The Bible talks about three different kinds of faith. I call these 'conversion', 'continuing' and 'charismatic' faith. Let me explain what these are.

1. CONVERSION FAITH

Conversion faith is the faith that saves you. Conversion faith is experienced when you believe in Jesus for the very first time – believing that he's the Son of God, that he died for your sins, that he rose again, and that he's alive forever.

The Bible teaches that this kind of faith is not just intellectual (giving assent to certain truths about Jesus), it is *relational* – it is a matter of putting your trust in a person who lived two thousand years ago. Conversion faith is intensely personal. It is a matter of deciding to trust in Jesus for the rest of your life and to follow him wherever he leads.

I experienced conversion faith in 1977. I was at a school which, when I arrived, was almost completely devoid of any authentic Christianity. By the time I left, a huge number of pupils had come to know Jesus. It was a remarkable season of genuine revival.

When this revival broke out I was most definitely not a Christian. I was far away from God and I was one of the most rebellious pupils in the school. But one night – in January 1977 – I was walking down a street and I sensed God speaking to me, inaudibly but powerfully. One moment I didn't believe in Jesus. The next moment I did. I confessed my sin and – amidst the tears – told Jesus that I truly believed in him. I put my trust in someone who is very real but currently invisible.

Everything changed for me that night. The next morning I woke up more alive than I'd ever felt. And I knew I had been forgiven – totally, instantly and unconditionally.

Have you ever experienced conversion faith?

....
....
....
....
....
....
....

If you have never exercised conversion faith, say this prayer with me now:

Dear Lord Jesus, I admit to you that I'm a sinner, that I have lived my life on my own terms not God's, and that I have ignored and even rejected your great love for me. I humbly ask for your forgiveness for my self-centredness. Thank you for dying on the cross so that I could be forgiven. I ask you to forgive me now and to enter my heart by your Holy Spirit and to be Lord of my life. Fill me with your love as I seek to follow and serve you to the end of my life, Amen.

2. CONTINUING FAITH

If you just prayed that prayer for the first time, or prayed a similar prayer in the past, then you have exercised conversion faith. However, this is not the last time you will exercise faith. You will need to continue to exercise faith, until your last breath. This brings me to 'continuing' faith.

The truth is we need to go on believing that Jesus is real, that he's alive, that he's all-powerful, that he's divine and that he's our Saviour and friend. We don't just put our trust in him once, at the time of our conversion. We have to go on putting our trust in him every day. We have to go on believing in him. We have to go on believing in his promises.

When I was studying John's Gospel, I discovered that the noun 'faith' is never used in the entire Gospel. That may seem strange to you, given that there is so much about believing in Jesus in the fourth Gospel. But it's absolutely true. At no point in the entire Gospel is the noun 'faith' used.

The verb 'believe' is, on the other hand, used frequently. Perhaps the classic example is the well-known verse, John 3:16: *'God so loved the world that he gave his one and only Son, that whoever believes in him shall not perish but have eternal life.'* Notice how John uses the verb 'believe' rather than the noun 'faith'. This is because faith is something *active* in his mind. It is something we do and go on doing. It is something that we have to activate and keep activating in our lives.

Faith as a noun sounds static. Believing as a verb sounds constant. In the mind of John the Evangelist, faith is something that has to be exercised all the time. So it's not just the case that I needed conversion faith to become a Christian. I also need continuing faith in order to keep living an authentic Christian life. So this morning I exercised continuing faith when I woke up and chose to go on believing that Jesus is real and that he's the Lord of my life. I exercised continuing faith as I prayed for others, that Jesus would be real to them and would meet their needs. I am exercising continuing faith right now that Jesus is guiding my thoughts and my hands as I write this book, and that he is blessing you as you read it.

We can't do without continuing faith. And this is of course a challenge. Sometimes we have to face hardship, trials, persecution and the like. Sometimes our lives are not like a smooth sea but a raging storm. In these times we need to go on believing. We need to activate and indeed go on activating our faith. As the Apostle Peter put it in 1 Peter 1:6–9:

In all this you greatly rejoice, though now for a little while you may have had to suffer grief in all kinds of trials. These have come so that the proven genuineness of your faith – of greater worth than gold, which perishes even though refined by fire – may result in praise, glory and honour when Jesus Christ is revealed. Though you have not seen him, you love him; and even though you do not see him now, you believe in him and are filled with an inexpressible and glorious joy, for you are receiving the end result of your faith, the salvation of your souls.

Continuing faith is so important. And without it, it is impossible to please God (Hebrews 11:6). Our continuing faith makes our heavenly Father really happy – and anything that makes him happy, we should actively pursue. Those who exercise 'continuing' faith will sooner or later discover that even though times may sometimes be very dark, the sun eventually rises.

Have you ever experienced a time when you felt like giving up – when things were so difficult you felt like you couldn't believe much longer?

....

....

....

....

....

3. CHARISMATIC FAITH

In addition to conversion and continuing faith the New Testament talks about a third kind of faith – what I call 'charismatic' faith.

Remember that the word 'charismatic' means 'grace gift'. Charismatic faith is the supernatural capacity to believe that God is about to move in a very special way to reveal his glory.

The Apostle Paul hints at this kind of faith in 1 Corinthians 13:2 when he writes:

> If I have the gift of prophecy and can fathom all mysteries and all knowledge, and if I have a faith that can move mountains, but do not have love, I am nothing.

Notice the phrase 'faith that can move mountains'. This seems to be more than conversion faith and more than continuing faith. This seems to me to be a very special kind of faith – charismatic faith or the gift of faith. This is a kind of faith that is in addition to the faith that saves us and the faith that we need for everyday Christian living.

All this should remind us of something that Jesus said about faith in Mark 11:22–23:

> 'Have faith in God,' Jesus answered. 'Truly I tell you, if anyone says to this mountain, "Go, throw yourself into the sea," and does not doubt in their heart but believes that what they say will happen, it will be done for them.'

If we want a useful definition of charismatic faith we might describe it figuratively as 'mountain-moving faith'. The gift of faith comes to us when there's a mountain that needs moving in our lives.

So what did Jesus and Paul mean by 'the mountain'?

The mountain is a word picture – it's a metaphor for anything that masquerades as an impossible difficulty in our lives. It's something that looms large in front of us, casting its shadow over everything we do, obscuring our view of the landscape of hope that lies before us.

This mountain can be a relational problem. It can be a financial difficulty. It can be a serious health issue. It can be a great concern for an issue of justice. It can be anything that looks like an insurmountable problem in your life. Jesus says that we are to believe God in these situations.

When a mountain looms large in front of us, Jesus wants us to exercise charismatic faith. He doesn't want us to behave like orphans and tell God how big our mountain is. He wants us to behave like royal sons and daughters and tell the mountain how big our God is. That's special faith!

Perhaps you can see now why charismatic faith is an essential spiritual gift. It is a vital tool in our utility belts as Christians. We cannot do anything extraordinary let alone heroic for our heavenly Father without from time to time receiving and using this gift. No insurmountable difficulty was ever overcome without extraordinary faith.

Maybe there is some great trial you are facing right now as you read this. Let me encourage you to look at that mountain – that redundancy, that cancer, that disaster, that loss – and say, 'You may seem overpoweringly great in my life right now, but I declare that my God is greater still. You are not going to conquer me. I am going to conquer you, through my faith in the One who is greater, higher and stronger. With his help, you will be hurled into the sea and your shadow will no longer envelop me in the darkness of despair. You will go and I will stay and my testimony will be to decree, "Look what the Lord has done for me!"'

What am I going to do as a result of what I've learned in this chapter?

....

....

....

....

....

....

....

....

....

....

....

....

....

....

4

THE HEALING GIFTS

To another is given gifts of healing by that one Spirit.

1 Corinthians 12:9

> The gift of healing is the supernatural ability to bring divine
> life and health to people suffering from physical, emotional
> and spiritual sickness.

I have always warmed to those who believe in the marriage of the
Word and the Spirit. It seems to me that the most authentic expressions of Christianity tend to happen among people who honour the
Bible and who welcome the Spirit. Jesus chastised people in his own
time for being ignorant of the Scriptures and the power of God. Today
he is looking for a people who know their Bibles and who welcome
the supernatural power of the Spirit.

When I became a Christian at the age of 16 it would be fair to say
that the group that I joined in those early years revered the Bible but
didn't have the same reverence for the supernatural gifts of the Holy
Spirit. Gifts like healing and miracles were said to have ceased at the
end of the New Testament era (a view known as 'cessationism') and
gifts like prophecy were interpreted as preaching. Although I learned
a lot from these teachers, their version of Christianity neglected the
gifts of the Spirit. In fact, in many ways they redefined the Trinity so
that it was 'the Father, the Son and the Holy Bible'.

Then I began to hear about a pastor from the USA called John Wimber. He had come over to the UK in 1981 to an Anglican church that later, in 1996, I would be called to lead – St Andrew's Chorley-wood. John had preached on Pentecost Sunday at St Andrew's and there had been an outpouring of the Holy Spirit, with people receiving remarkable healings and other signs of God's manifest presence.

A few years later, in 1983, I began training for the ordained ministry in the Church of England. I did this at a theological college in the UK doing a fast-tracked degree in theology and biblical studies at the local university.

Halfway through that time I was invited to go to the City Hall in Sheffield to hear John Wimber talk about signs, wonders and the kingdom of God. At first I was reluctant to go because I had bought into the view that 'signs and wonders' may have been visible in the first-century church but they aren't visible today.

How wrong I was!

I will never forget that week as long as I live. It rocked my theology and changed my life. From the first session on the Monday to the last session on the Thursday John Wimber undermined all my objections and broke through all my intellectual defences. I simply couldn't argue with his excellent teaching.

The whole week was thoroughly Christ-centred and Bible-based. More than that, it was totally saturated in the Spirit of God. To be perfectly honest, I had never heard anyone teach that the gifts of the Holy Spirit were meant to be operative throughout church history. I had never heard anyone make the case so compellingly that gifts like healing and miraculous works are normative demonstrations of the reality of the kingdom of God and that we are to expect them today. It was clear, simple, biblical and rigorous. More than that, it was backed up with evidence.

In fact, I had never come across anyone like John Wimber, teaching from the Word that the gifts of the Spirit can be experienced today and then confirming the truth of that with demonstrations of power. Every time John spoke, he would follow his talk by waiting on the Holy Spirit, listening for prophetic words, and then praying for the sick. Hundreds of people testified that they had received divine healing.

By the end of the conference I was able to testify that for the first time I had prayed for someone and seen them healed. I went to an afternoon seminar on how to minister healing in Jesus' name. When the teaching concluded, we were all invited to pray for people in the room who needed healing.

The model of prayer we were taught was a simple one:

Step 1: Interview (finding out the person's name and their need)
Step 2: Diagnosis (listening to the person and the Father and
    diagnosing the real need, not just the presented need)
Step 3: Prayer selection (determining how to pray)
Step 4: Prayer (finding out what the Father is doing and then praying
    into that)
Step 5: Post-prayer direction (encouraging the person to walk out
    their healing)

Many of the people at the workshop were encouraged to pray for someone who needed healing. I was allocated a person who had one leg shorter than the other. One of John Wimber's team talked me through the process, including asking the person whether they wanted the longer leg to be shortened or the shorter leg to be lengthened (something I would never have thought of asking). Then I began to pray in the name of Jesus, commanding the short leg to lengthen. And I watched in absolute amazement as the shorter leg grew visibly in front of my eyes until both legs were exactly the same length and the person was able to stand with perfect balance for the first time.

I don't think anyone was more surprised than me (although the person receiving prayer was obviously shocked and delighted).

From that moment on I knew I was never going to be the same. I knew that proclamation needed to be backed up with demonstration. The Word needed to be confirmed with signs and wonders.

Now here's the interesting thing. It just so happened that I was writing an essay that week for my theology degree. I was set some reading and the primary textbook was a work by a New Testament scholar who had tried his best to argue that the stories of healing in the Gospels were fictional. What an irony! While reading a book denying God's healing power I attended a conference which provided a terminal critique of it. I'm afraid the book went in the bin and I was from that conference on convinced that Jesus Christ is the same yesterday, today and forever, and that he healed the sick 2,000 years ago and he heals the sick today.

Do you believe that God heals the sick today?

....

....

....

....

....

....

....

Let's look again at the Apostle Paul's teaching about the gifts of the Holy Spirit in 1 Corinthians 12:7–11:

Now to each one the manifestation of the Spirit is given for the common good. To one there is given through the Spirit a message of wisdom, to another a message of knowledge by means of the same Spirit, to another faith by the same Spirit, to another gifts of healing by that one Spirit, to another miraculous powers, to another prophecy, to another distinguishing between spirits, to another speaking in different kinds of tongues, and to still another the interpretation of tongues. All these are the work of one and the same Spirit, and he distributes them to each one, just as he determines.

We come now to the fourth of the nine gifts of the Holy Spirit, called 'gifts of healing'.

The phrase in the original language of the New Testament is *charismata hiamaton*. *Charismata* means 'grace gifts' and *hiamaton* means 'healings'. Both words are in the plural. So this gift could justifiably be translated as 'gifts of healings'.

As we explore this gift, I want to emphasize a number of key ideas.

1. GENEROSITY

Please note that out of all the nine gifts this is the only one which is specifically prefaced by the word *charismata*. The word '*charismata*' contains the word *charis* which can be translated as 'grace'. 'Grace' means two things to the Christian. It first of all denotes the unmerited love of God, demonstrated in the saving work of Christ on the cross. Then it denotes the empowering work of the Holy Spirit in a believer's life, enabling them to do far more than they could ever do on their own. In both cases, the word points to the generosity of a loving, heavenly Father. It points to the fact that we cannot save ourselves but that God in Christ has done that for us. It points to the truth that we cannot achieve the Father's destiny in our own strength but that he has given us the power to fulfil his purposes.

When Paul calls healing 'a grace gift', he emphasizes very strongly that this gift is completely and unreservedly the work of God. Those who have a special gift for praying for sick people to recover can never say that this is a gift that derives from their capabilities or from their worthiness. It is emphatically something that comes from the Father. It is no indicator of their strengths or their spirituality. It is simply a sign of Abba Father's undeserved generosity.

2. MERCY

When we think of *charis* we think of the cross, and when we think of the cross we think of the most vivid demonstration of the Father's love. There is simply no greater display of the extreme mercy of God than the open arms of the dying Saviour at Calvary. The cross of Christ is the most beautiful and life-transforming reminder that God's mercy has triumphed over his judgement.

If judgement is getting what we deserve, then mercy is getting what we don't deserve. At Calvary, God remembered mercy. When the Apostle Paul took the trouble to say that healing gifts are signs of God's grace, he was reminding us of the Father's mercy.

With that in mind, it stands to reason that the primary motivation of the person endowed with the healing gifts should be mercy and compassion. The character of the gifted person needs to reflect the character of the gift itself. So the more you cultivate mercy, the more you'll release mercy.

Mercy and compassion have to be the engine that drives the healing gifts. In this respect, the adopted sons and daughters need to imitate the natural Son, Jesus of Nazareth. One of my favourite verses in the New Testament (Matthew 14:14) simply says this:

> *When Jesus landed and saw a large crowd, he had compassion on them and healed those who were ill.*

Jesus was compelled by love to pray for the sick. His motivation was mercy. He loved sick and broken people. We should always remember that the gifts of the Spirit are meant to be administered with love (1 Corinthians 13).

3. Variety

It's interesting that the Apostle Paul speaks about the gifts of healings (plural) rather than the gift of healing (singular).

Some argue from this that this means that the Holy Spirit gives different people in the body of Christ the anointing to heal specific conditions. So, one believer has the grace for healing bone disease, another has the grace to pray for the healing of blood disorders, another has the grace to pray for the healing of depression, another has the grace for the healing of relationships, another has the grace for the healing of memories, and so on.

But the grammar doesn't really allow for this interpretation. Paul says, 'to another [i.e. to another individual] is given gifts of healings'. One person (singular) has healing gifts (plural). What this indicates is that the one who is anointed with the healing gifts will find themselves being used by God to bring freedom to all sorts of different diseases and problems, not just one particular type of affliction.

On one occasion, the gifted person may find they are praying for someone to be delivered from evil spirits. On another they may find they are praying for someone's emotions to be healed. On another they may find they are praying for someone's arthritis to be cured. While they may have special faith for the healing of certain kinds of conditions, they will be called to a broad spectrum of prayer, from spiritual healing (deliverance), through emotional healing to physical healing.

Let me emphasize this point about variety. There are three main ways in which the healing gifts can be used:

- In physical healing – the healing of our bodies
- In spiritual healing – deliverance from evil spirits
- In emotional or inner healing – the healing of our hearts and minds

Most Christians can readily accept the need for physical healing, even if they don't see it as often as they would like.

Spiritual healing is more problematic. Some find it very hard to accept that Christians might need to be set free from the influence of evil spirits. Yet this is precisely what is required from time to time, especially if we suffer from demonic oppression and are being attacked by evil spirits. When this happens, those with healing gifts can pray for the tormented person to be set free in Jesus' name.

In addition to physical and spiritual healing, there is emotional or inner healing – the healing of a person's past hurts. Again, those with healing gifts are given a special grace for setting people free from the wounds that often lie behind destructive patterns of behaviour.

There is accordingly a variety of ways in which healing gifts can be used.

Which of these types of healing have you most often seen – physical, emotional or spiritual healing?

....

....

....

....

....

---

4. Sovereignty

It is vital at this point to emphasize what the Apostle Paul emphasizes, which is that it is the Holy Spirit who determines who receives the healing gifts in the body of Christ.

Towards the end of 1 Corinthians 12 Paul asks (in verse 30), '*Do all have gifts of healing?*' This is clearly a rhetorical question expecting the answer, 'No'. Paul recognized that not every member of the body of Christ has a special grace and anointing for seeing the sick healed.

While every believer is called to pray for the sick (as part of our commission to extend the kingdom of God throughout the earth), not every believer has a special gift in this area. We all have the authority as adopted, royal sons and daughters of God to command sickness to leave in Jesus' name. But not all of us have a recognized gift for effecting healings. For some of us, praying for healing is something we are called to do from time to time as we meet situations of need. Others are anointed to pray for the sick all the time.

This brings us to the idea of God's sovereignty – that God is the sole ruler over all things and that he alone is free to decide who receives the healing gifts in the body of Christ, the church. We cannot choose the gifts of healing as a child would pick a gift from the branches of a Christmas tree. It is the Holy Spirit who decides which believer receives which gifts. As the Apostle Paul writes in 1 Corinthians 12:11:

> *All these are the work of one and the same Spirit, and he distributes them to each one, just as he determines.*

That said, we should also remember that the Holy Spirit is profoundly attracted to our spiritual hunger. The gifts of the Spirit are for the passionate not for the passive. If you have a compassion for sick people, ask your Father for the healing gifts. If you are around sick people a great deal because of your profession or your circumstances, having this gift will be an immeasurable blessing to others. Provided you use it sensitively and respectfully, you will bring heaven to those who may be going through hell on earth. So ask for the healing gifts!

5. CONTINUITY

Every believer is called to pray for the sick as part of spreading the message and ministry of the kingdom worldwide. In making the

Good News of Jesus go viral, the ministry of divine healing will always prove essential.

At the same time, there are some believers who have a special grace for praying for the sick and seeing them supernaturally cured.

What's the difference between these two? Here we need to distinguish between fixed gifts and variable gifts.

All of us have a certain number of fixed gifts. These are permanent gifts that are a permanent component of our calling. At the same time, we can receive variable gifts – ones that are given for pressing situations and for passing needs.

Those given the healing gifts as part of their calling have these as fixed gifts. These are with them for the long haul, for the whole of their Christian lives. When Paul asks, 'Do all have gifts of healing?' it is important to note that the verb 'have' is in the present continuous. In other words, it means, 'Do all go on having the healing gifts?'

This is more than a matter of semantics. It points to the truth that those who receive the healing gifts as a fixed rather than a variable anointing will have them for the whole of their Christian lives. When the Father gives healing gifts to some of his children, these are supposed to be presents that form a permanent part of their ministry. These gifts have a built-in continuity to them. More than that, believers will continue to operate in these gifts until Jesus returns, at which point – in the new heavens and the new earth – there will be no more sickness and therefore no further need for healing. So there is continuity to the healing gifts, but this continuity is not eternal.

6. Humility

There is something interesting about the end of 1 Corinthians 12, the chapter on the gifts of the Spirit.

In reality there are many interesting things, but there's one in particular I'd like to highlight. Here's the passage, verses 27–31:

Now you are the body of Christ, and each one of you is a part of it. And God has placed in the church first of all apostles, second prophets, third teachers, then miracles, then gifts of healing, of helping, of guidance, and of different kinds of tongues. Are all apostles? Are all prophets? Are all teachers? Do all work miracles? Do all have gifts of healing? Do all speak in tongues? Do all interpret? Now eagerly desire the greater gifts.

What's noteworthy here is that Paul is comfortable talking about apostles, prophets and teachers. But when he comes in the next breath to miracles and healing he doesn't say 'miracle-workers and healers'. He speaks about the gifts rather than the gifted people and says, *'then miracles, then gifts of healing'.*

There may be a number of reasons for this but one is Paul's desire to keep believers walking in humility when it comes to the spiritual gifts. He knows that there are some in the church in Corinth who are using the more dramatic gifts (like healing and miracles) as evidence that they are more spiritual than those who don't. These people have very likely elevated themselves to the status of 'healers' and 'miracle-workers', leaving other members of the church – with gifts such as 'helping' and 'guidance' – feeling like second-class citizens in the kingdom.

Maybe you have felt like that at times in your Christian life?

Maybe others have made you feel that they are more anointed, more charismatic than you?

Paul knocks this pride on the head by refusing to talk about healers at all, or miracle-workers for that matter. He speaks instead about the gifts of healing and in the process reminds everyone that this gift does not make us faith healers or any other kind of healer.

There is only one healer in Paul's mind, that's Jesus.

If any of us have healing gifts, then it is because we have been given them so that we can continue the healing ministry of Jesus today.

Jesus is the healer. Give him the glory, not the person who has healing gifts.

7. MYSTERY

No one can operate in the healing gifts for long before confronting one of the biggest questions: 'Why do some people not get healed when we pray for them in the name of Jesus?'

There are no easy answers to this question. Many people argue that God chooses who gets healed and who doesn't and it's entirely his decision. We are the clay, he is the potter. It is his decision how we are shaped and when.

I have a friend, very gifted in praying for the healing of the sick, who takes this view and who says, 'When it comes to healing, I teach that it's up to God who gets healed when we pray for them. That way, when someone isn't healed, then I don't get the blame; when someone is healed, I don't get the glory.'

This on the surface sounds very reasonable. Yet what lies behind this view may not be quite as reasonable. For when you peel away the layers of this argument you find that it involves us believing in a God who only wants to heal some of the people some of the time. Yet how attractive and indeed biblical is that as a God-image?

The Bible teaches that Jesus Christ is the exact representation of God's likeness and being – that if we want to know what God is really like then we must look closely at Jesus. He who has seen Jesus has seen the Father.

When we look at Jesus we discover that he healed everyone who came to him and asked and he healed them of every kind of disease. If this is true, then how does this challenge the view that God wants to heal some of the people some of the time? I would have to say that it deals it a fairly crushing blow. For if Jesus wanted to heal every person who asked, and of every disease, then that is surely what the Father wants too.

How do you react when someone you pray for is not healed?

....

....

....

....

....

....

....

The issue of why some are not healed is a very deep and perplexing one. However, our reaction to the mystery of unanswered prayer is absolutely crucial. In many ways it will determine whether we grow in the anointing of healing or not.

Whenever someone we pray for is not healed we are faced with two main options.

The first is to react in the flesh and become disillusioned. While this is perfectly understandable it also has dangerous consequences. More often than not it leads to cynicism. It may even lead to us not praying for the sick again.

The second option is to respond in the Spirit and become combative. What I mean by this is that instead of dialling down on praying for the sick we can do the opposite. We can contend even more fervently for the very area where we have seen a temporary setback.

Let me give you an example of what I mean.

I remember one of my friends in ministry being diagnosed with lung cancer. Some of the most gifted people I know (especially in the area of healing and miracles) prayed for him, both interceding from afar and laying hands on him in his home. Yet he did not recover. He died at a relatively young age.

Not long afterwards people came from far and near to the thanksgiving service. There were many powerful moments in that service, but there were none perhaps more powerful than right at the end, when the man's son asked his mother if he could say something.

I'll let the son tell you in his own words what happened, in a personal message he sent to me afterwards:

> At the end of the funeral I spoke about how I did not know why my dad died but I did know that God is faithful and wants to heal.
>
> Then I said I wanted to pray for everyone who was sick and needed a miracle. I prayed for one lady who had a condition called 'black lung disease'. Her doctor had told her if she did not receive a miracle it would turn into lung cancer.
>
> I prayed for her and when she went back to the doctor the next week, the doctor told her that there were no more signs of the black lung and she was completely healed.

Now that's what I call 'responding in the Spirit' when disappointment strikes and when mystery confronts us.

That son didn't become cynical. Instead he chose to fight for the very condition that his father had died from.

That's faith.

The son's mother related to me her version of this event as well:

> At the very end of the funeral our youngest son wanted to say something. I thought he was going to talk about his dad. He said, 'We have no idea why Dad was not healed on this earth but Father still heals. So I want to pray for those of you with cancer in your bodies, especially lung cancer or lung conditions.'
>
> This lady had been diagnosed with black lung syndrome. She grew up around coal mines. My son prayed for her.

For years we never heard back from her directly. We didn't know her name but we had heard stories about a lady who had been prayed for, so we knew she existed and that she had been healed.

I was doing some meetings three years later and spoke about her during one of my talks. I mentioned that a lady came up for healing at the funeral and that I would love to know what happened to her.

Unbeknown to me that lady was in the audience. She came up after the talk and told me that when she had gone back to the doctor he X-rayed her and there was no sign of disease. She had been healed.

Since then she had spent some time out of the country, so that is why we never heard. She told me that she had emailed me but I never received it.

She is now on my ministry team. Isn't that amazing?

If there's a spectrum from active faith to passive scepticism, where would you locate yourself on it right now?

....

....

....

....

....

....

Now I tell this story for a reason.

Several years later I was asked to speak at a thanksgiving service for a young member of the church where I was the pastor. She had been a very godly young woman and a very popular teacher at one of our local schools. Very shortly after she got married it was discovered she had cancer.

During the next nine years she fought this condition with extraordinary courage and great faith. We had every anointed man and woman of God that we could possibly think of pray for her healing. But she did not receive a miracle cure. She died very peacefully.

Her husband – a wonderful young man of God – asked me to speak at the thanksgiving service. On the morning of the funeral, I woke up feeling disappointed that God hadn't healed her and – if I'm honest – a bit downhearted too.

Then I started thinking of my friend who had also died of cancer and as I did I suddenly remembered the brave stand that his son had made for healing at his father's funeral.

I wrote to both the son and the mother and they responded straight away with the messages you've just read. These messages filled me with faith . . . fighting faith.

From that moment I knew what my heavenly Father wanted me to do. He wanted me to do the opposite of what the natural mind would lead me to do. He wanted me to pray for miracles at a service remembering someone who hadn't received one.

So after sharing the testimony of what the son had done, I asked those who had cancer to raise a hand. Out of hundreds of people, I saw at least twenty people respond.

I prayed a simple prayer, asking that Jesus would heal someone miraculously. I commanded cancer to leave people's bodies in Jesus' mighty name.

I can't say a lot here about what happened next, because of confidentiality, but I heard later of at least one young woman who had been struggling with her faith through some very dark days.

As soon as she raised her hand she became acutely aware of her heart racing and her body beginning to shake. She felt the sensation of her blood flowing round her chest.

A few days later she had a dream in which she saw herself in the midst of a fierce storm. She heard the Father saying to her, 'Heaven isn't ready for you yet.' This whole experience gave her enormous strength and brought her very close to the Father – at a time when she had been sorely tried.

Now I can't confirm yet whether this young woman has received healing. That in a sense is not the reason I am telling this story – though I hope you'll join me in praying that her body is completely cancer-free, in Jesus' name.

The reason I'm sharing this testimony is because all of us have a choice when it comes to unanswered prayer. We can react in the flesh and stop praying for healing or we can respond in the Spirit and fight with faith for the very issue where we've seen a setback.

We can either be overwhelmed by the mystery of unanswered prayer or we can become radically intentional about pursuing more of the miraculous. We can focus on what God has not done or we can build our faith on what he has done. When mystery comes, it's our choice.

To what extent is your view of healing dictated by what God has not done rather than what he has done?

....

....

....

....

....

....

In conclusion, I want to add that I passionately believe that the healing gifts are designed to be a normal part of the church's life and ministry.

Keep in mind that Paul is writing about Christians when they gather together to worship when he mentions the gifts of healing in 1 Corinthians 12. As far as Paul is concerned, there should always be space made for those with gifts of healing to pray for the sick when Christians meet to worship God.

The church is called to be a family of people that care deeply for each other's physical, emotional and spiritual well-being. When Christians assemble, one of the indications that they are a genuine biblical family is that the sick are healed. Every church should cultivate a kingdom culture in which broken hearts are mended and diseased bodies are healed. Every church should give space for the gifts of healing.

One of the things that I think would shock the Apostle Paul most if he visited many churches today is the lack of such signs of God's presence in public worship. Demonstrations of God's power – especially through healing – are part and parcel of the church's normal life.

To return to a point I made at the start of this chapter, all those who follow Jesus today need to seek to bring together the Word and the Spirit. The Father is looking for people who know the Scriptures and who also know the power of God.

The great healing evangelist Smith Wigglesworth talked about and modelled this union of the Word and the Spirit in his remarkable ministry in the first half of the twentieth century. Shortly before he died in 1947, he received a prophetic word about the future of the church in the UK. He wrote:

When the Word and the Spirit come together, there will be the biggest move of the Holy Spirit that the nations, and indeed the world have ever seen. It will mark the beginning of a revival that will eclipse anything that has been witnessed within these shores, even the Wesleyan and Welsh revivals of former years.

If ever there was a time to honour the Bible and to welcome the gifts of the Spirit (including healing) it is today.

Let's restore the healing gifts to the church's life and ministry, and let's do this in a biblical way – a way that glorifies Jesus.

What am I going to do as a result of what I've learned in this chapter?

....

....

....

....

....

....

....

....

....

....

....

....

....

5

THE GIFT OF MIRACLES

To another is given the gift of miraculous powers.

1 Corinthians 12:10

> The gift of miracles is the God-given capacity to perform supernatural signs which fill people with wonder.

I want to introduce you to a remarkable man. He is a Norwegian called Tjor Kjell (pronounced Tor Shell) and he witnessed the most wonderful miracle in his son's life.

In May 2002, Tjor Kjell and his wife Eva received a telephone call from Thailand in which they heard the news that their son Per Arne had been involved in a serious car accident. Per Arne had flown to Bangkok to visit a friend. The two of them had been driving to the north of Thailand to a wedding when their car was involved in a head-on collision with several other cars. Per Arne was very seriously injured.

Per Arne and his friend were with YWAM (Youth with a Mission) at that time. Some members of YWAM in Thailand were alerted to the crash and they went with Per Arne to the hospital in Bangkok, a journey of six hours. Per Arne's eyes had rolled over white by the time they arrived, a sign that he was dying.

Tjor Kjell and Eva immediately got on the first plane out to Thailand and arrived to find that their son was in a hospital bed with a tube in his mouth. He was in a coma and the doctors told them that there was no hope. They had conducted some scans and there was a lot of bleeding in the brain. Per Arne was breathing only twice every minute. It looked like it would only be a matter of days before he died.

However, when she entered the hospital room, Eva had seen an angel – as tall as the ceiling of the room – leaning over Per Arne's bed, with his face looking into Per Arne's face. The angel was dressed for war and at that moment Eva knew that he was fighting for her son and she felt a deep peace that this was not the end; that her son would live.

Back home in Oslo the family prayed. People began to pray all over Norway and increasingly all over the world. Per Arne was lying in a hospital bed in a coma, paralysed, with a broken neck, barely breathing. It seemed like there was no hope.

On the way out to Thailand, Tjor Kjell had remembered some words from a worship song 'What a Faithful God'. Now, at his son's bedside, he was faced with two realities. The reality of earth was that his son was almost certainly going to die. If he lived, the doctors had told him that he would never be a normal person again. The reality of heaven was that nothing is too hard for the Lord. Indeed the presence of an angel in the room had revealed that heaven had already invaded his son's life.

On 9 May 2002 Tjor Kjell received a striking prophetic word:

The church in Norway is in a coma, just as your son is in a coma. But the church in Norway is going to wake up, and as a sign to you that this is going to happen I will awaken your son from his coma. The church in Norway will have an awakening, especially among young boys and girls.

As Tjor Kjell heard these words he was deeply moved. He sensed that God was speaking to him 'father to father', as it were. Just as

Tjor Kjell was desperate for connection, contact and communication with his son, so our heavenly Father is desperate for the same depth of intimacy with his people. Later Tjor Kjell was to say that at that moment he became profoundly aware of the Father's passion for us, for his intense desire to be a loving Father to us all.

As this encounter drew to a close, Tjor Kjell heard these amazing words, 'You will see Per Arne get up on Pentecost Sunday.' Pentecost Sunday was eleven days away (20 May)!

Over the next week, Per Arne's condition deteriorated dramatically. The news from the doctors got worse and worse. Worship songs were played and sung day and night in Per Arne's room. Prayers went up there and all over the world. After seven days the MRI scan revealed that Per Arne's brain was worse than before. There was still a lot of bleeding and the damage was greater than was at first thought.

Then, on 19 May, the day before Pentecost Sunday, Per Arne seemed to be on the edge of death. His face went blue, his blood pressure dropped and he developed a fever.

A ferocious storm began to brew outside the hospital. There were loud cracks of thunder and a lot of lightning. Both the father and the mother realized that there was a fierce battle going on for Per Arne's life.

The doctor in charge that night ushered Tjor Kjell out of the room saying that Per Arne was going to die and that there was nothing more anyone could do. He needed to let the medics attend to his son from now on.

Tjor Kjell remembered the story of Lazarus. It was nearly midnight, Pentecost Sunday. He knew that nothing was impossible for the Lord and that the same Jesus who raised Lazarus could raise his son, even now.

At that moment the doctor rushed back and told him to come quickly. Something remarkable was happening and he needed to be with Per Arne right away.

When Tjor Kjell went into the room, Per Arne's eyes were open. He had woken up. He was breathing normally without a tube in his mouth and throat. Like Lazarus, Per Arne had been awakened.

Tjor Kjell had got his son back.

And the doctor – a Buddhist – was exclaiming, 'This is a miracle! This is a miracle! Your God is the true God!'

A week or so later, Per Arne returned to Norway. A Norwegian consultant conducted some MRI scans on him and compared them with the MRI scans that had been done in Bangkok just a week before.

He said, 'This cannot be true. I do not believe this is your son. We have never seen anything like this before.'

Since then Per Arne has shared his testimony many times. He presents people with three options after he has told his remarkable story:

- **Option 1:** You believe that the whole story is made up and therefore untrue.
- **Option 2:** You believe that there is a kernel of truth but it has been exaggerated.
- **Option 3:** You believe that it did happen and that God is alive and does miracles.

Per Arne's testimony is: 'I was almost dead and God woke me up!'

His wife Monika – who interceded for Per Arne's healing before she had even met or knew him – says this: 'God has done this as an example of what he can do. Per Arne's miracle is a reminder that we have a big God and that nothing is too hard for the Lord.'

Have you ever witnessed a miracle?

....

....

....

....

....

....

....

In this chapter we turn to the gift of miraculous works.

In the original language, this particular spiritual gift is described by Paul in two words. The first word is *energemata*, from which we get 'energy' and 'energize'. This carries the idea of supernatural empowerment. It reminds us that to work miracles is not a natural talent but a supernatural gift. When miracles happen, they happen because of spiritual power not physical strength.

The second word is *dunameis*, which literally means 'powers'. It is the word from which we get 'dynamite'. Although we should be careful not to make too much of this, it is important to understand that the gift of miraculous works is a manifestation of the extraordinary power of the Holy Spirit.

So the gift we're looking at in this chapter is described by Paul in a double plural – literally 'workings of powers'.

This compact expression points to two important truths.

Firstly, these 'powers' are not any old powers. They are not the destructive powers that the devil has at his disposal. They are not mystical force fields within the natural order either. Nor are they the human powers men and women are endowed with. Rather, they are the many different expressions of divine power performed by the

Holy Spirit. They are evidence of the power that is released when we pray in the name of Jesus.

Secondly, when Paul uses the word 'workings' he points to the different ways in which these displays of power can be made manifest. Clearly in Paul's mind the word 'miracles' covers a rich and broad spectrum of supernatural happenings. Miracles are not restricted to one simple phenomenon, such as dramatic and wonder-evoking works of physical healing. They can cover a wide range of events, from raising the dead to multiplying food.

In summary, then:

- Paul understood that the adopted sons and daughters of God were to continue the ministry of Jesus and that this involved working miracles.
- He didn't define 'workings of miracles' but he would have seen them as displays of heavenly power which bring glory to Jesus.
- He recognized that there was diversity in relation to these supernatural acts, which is why he used the double plural 'workings of powers'.
- He was adamant that these displays of power were the work of the Holy Spirit and not the expression of some indefinable spiritual force.
- He knew that some members of the body of Christ were anointed with a special ability to perform such mighty deeds.
- He believed that these people were endowed by the Holy Spirit for this ministry and that this was a sign not of their spirituality but of God's generosity.
- He also contended that believers who worked miracles were to do so not for their own glorification but for the common good and to strengthen the church.

Do you know any Christians who have a special ability to do mighty works which bring glory to Jesus?

....

....

....

....

....

....

Before we look at the varieties of miraculous experience, it might be helpful and constructive to understand what miracles really are. Here's my definition:

> Miracles are extraordinary events that can't be explained using scientific categories, which are attributed to the more unusual actions of God, and which cause both believers and unbelievers to stand in awe of God's mercy or his judgement.

Let's just unravel this statement.

1. MIRACLES ARE EXTRAORDINARY EVENTS

In other words, they do not happen every day in our experience as believers. They are unusual displays of power in the regular routines of life.

This is an important point. We must always remember that miracles are exceptional events which evoke awe. If the exceptional became normal then our awe would decrease and the word 'miracle' would lose its currency.

2. THESE EVENTS CANNOT BE EXPLAINED USING SCIENTIFIC CATEGORIES

This is especially true with dramatic, sudden, remarkable healing events. These always defy medical explanation

So with Per Arne's story, the Norwegian doctor back home, seeing the MRI scans of the brain before and after the miracle, couldn't believe it was the same person and admitted that he and his team had never seen anything like it before.

Miracles are not reducible to easy scientific explanations.

3. MIRACLES ARE ATTRIBUTED TO THE ACTIONS OF GOD

They are evidence of God's continuing involvement in the world that he has created. They are exceptional signs of his commitment to restore people and renew the planet.

Let's remember at this point that there are three basic world-views that people often adopt when it comes to God and creation.

There is of course atheism. Atheists do not believe in God. They therefore do not believe that God created the world and they certainly do not believe that he continues to be involved in the world.

There is also deism. Deists believe in a creator God but they do not believe he continues to act within his creation. God is like a watchmaker. He has made the watch but he lets the watch now run on its own.

Then there is theism. Theists believe in God as creator and they also believe that God continues to work within the created order. Miracles are dramatic illustrations or signs of this continuing involvement.

In the Christian worldview God is the most loving Father in the universe.

He is a living Father, not a dead or non-existent Father (contra atheism).

He is a very involved Father, not an absent Father (contra deism).

He is a Father who loves his creation and has the power and the desire to mend what has become broken.

Our heavenly Abba has the power to save, heal and deliver human beings and indeed the whole of creation.

4. MIRACLES CAUSE BOTH BELIEVERS AND UNBELIEVERS TO STAND IN AWE OF GOD

The whole point about supernatural signs is that they cause us to marvel at the greatness of God. That is why they are often called 'wonders'.

When believers see miraculous works, it causes them to worship God for his glory and his greatness. It increases their capacity to believe that nothing is too hard for the Lord – that nothing is impossible for God.

When unbelievers see such things, they sometimes do what the Buddhist doctor did in Per Arne's testimony. They proclaim, 'This is a miracle! This is a miracle! Your God is the true God!'

Miracles are therefore essential in witnessing to unbelievers.

5. MIRACLES POINT EITHER TO GOD'S JUDGEMENT OR TO HIS MERCY

We need to realize here that some miracles demonstrate God's judgement.

Let's take an example from the ministry of a remarkable man of God called Mahesh Chavda.

When Mahesh was preaching the gospel in Zaire, he came across a tree known as 'The Sorcerer's Tree'. A number of sorcerers had been meeting around this tree to put curses on Mahesh and the Christians in the area as they met nearby.

Suddenly fire appeared in the sky, streaking from the area of the meeting and falling upon the tree, burning it from the top to the ground. The leaves and branches were totally destroyed by the fire, leaving only a part of the trunk. This tree had originally stood thirty feet tall.

This was a miracle which demonstrated God's judgement.

In this respect, we must remember that God is not just a loving Father. He is also a righteous Father and when he sees things like sorcery, he finds it detestable, according to Deuteronomy 18:10–13. Furthermore, he judges what he detests.

When it comes to the miraculous, we need to remember that we have a heavenly Father whose miracles sometimes reveal his judgement, not just his mercy.

Most miracles are creative. But some can be miracles that bring death, not life.

> **How do you respond to the thought that we have a Father whose power can reveal his judgement not just his mercy?**
>
> ....
>
> ....
>
> ....
>
> ....
>
> ....
>
> ....

Before we look at the variety of miracles that are covered by this spiritual gift it is important to identify the difference between the gift of healing (which I described in the last chapter) and the gift of miracles.

This is all the more urgent because I have begun this chapter on miracles with a testimony of healing. Does this mean that healing and miracles are the same?

It's here that we need to remember there is an overlap between some of the gifts and that the distinctions are not hard and fast but sometimes fluid. So, for example, there is evidently some overlap between wisdom and knowledge; both involve the giving of spiritual insight. The same is true of the gift of healing and the gift of miraculous works. Some examples of physical healing fall into the territory occupied by miracles.

When someone is healed dramatically, visibly, conclusively, suddenly and totally, I would argue that this can legitimately be described as a miracle.

Per Arne's marvellous recovery could be described as an example of the gift of healing; but it more readily lends itself to the language of the miraculous.

Some physical healings are therefore miracles. But not all miracles are physical healings.

Do you think that dramatic physical healings should be regarded as examples of the gift of miraculous works?

....

....

....

....

....

....

As we continue to study the gift of miraculous powers, we move now to the broad diversity of supernatural events that this gift covers.

I would maintain that there are at least seven types of miraculous works – which again would explain why the Apostle Paul uses a double plural with this gift.

1. MIRACLES OF RESURRECTION

These are miracles in which a believer prays for a dead person to be revived in the name of Jesus.

Jesus himself raised people from the dead, most notably the daughter of Jairus, the son of the widow of Nain, and the brother of Mary and Martha, Lazarus. All three were raised from the dead instantly and publicly.

These resurrections were not permanent (because the people concerned would one day die again) and so they are really 'resuscitation miracles'. Nonetheless, this in no way diminishes their awe-evoking power.

2. MIRACLES OF NATURE

Jesus performed miracles which involved dramatic transformations of nature.

For example, he stilled a raging storm on the Sea of Galilee through a single command (Mark 4:39).

He transformed the water in six earthenware vessels into approximately 600 litres (180 gallons) of fine wine (John 2:1–11).

He walked on the deep waters of Galilee without sinking (John 6:16–24).

Jesus clearly performed nature miracles.

There are times when God calls believers to issue a command which influences and transforms aspects of nature. Those who have the gift of miraculous works have the capacity in situations of desperate need to command storms to still and rain to fall.

3. MIRACLES OF DELIVERANCE

Jesus performed mighty acts of deliverance. Sometimes these are referred to as exorcisms. The Gospels of Matthew, Mark and Luke portray many such miracles in the ministry of Jesus. There is no doubt that these Gospels faithfully record a vital part of the work of the historical Jesus.

The Bible teaches that we are caught up in a spiritual war between the kingdom of God and the powers of darkness. There were many people at the time of Jesus who were oppressed by the devil.

Many people are tormented by demonic spirits today, especially as a result of their personal involvement with the occult. When someone is dramatically and visibly set free from such torment, it can justly be said that they have received a miracle.

4. MIRACLES OF JUDGEMENT

The most obvious example of this in the ministry of Jesus is when he was walking past a fig tree outside Jerusalem and felt hungry. There were many leaves but no figs. Jesus then spoke a word of judgement to the tree, causing it to wither from the roots and die. The next day the disciples noticed this dramatic transformation and asked Jesus how he had done this. He then taught about having faith in God and not doubting when we stand and pray (Mark 11:12–26).

From time to time a believer with the gift of miraculous works may be called upon to speak a word that brings judgement.

It should be noted, however, that the judging of the fig tree was not just a physical miracle; it was also a symbolic act.

Keep in mind that the fig tree is a symbol of Israel in the Bible.

Jesus had come to his own people, the people of Israel, and they had rejected him (John 1:10–11). His judgement of the fig tree needs to be seen in the light of Jesus' rebuke to many of the Jewish people of his day (especially the Jewish authorities in Jerusalem). Just after he judges the fig tree, Jesus enters the temple in Jerusalem and finds that the temple is full of people but it is also full of corruption. Like the fig tree, there is the appearance of life but no fruit. Like the fig tree, the temple has proved to be unproductive. So Jesus casts out the money changers and the animal sellers in an act of righteous anger.

The miracle of judgement involving the fig tree is accordingly part of a sequence of events and mustn't be seen in isolation.

Any miracle of judgement today is going to be a sign of God's judgement of spiritual blindness, demonic wickedness and social injustice.

When the sorcerer's tree was burned from top to bottom it was a dramatic and visible symbol of God's anger against demonic wickedness.

5. MIRACLES OF PROVISION

The most memorable example of this in the Gospels is when Jesus multiplies five small loaves and two fish into enough food to feed five thousand men. This story is recorded by all four Gospels and is clearly based in fact. The Gospel writers all conclude by saying that everyone who ate was satisfied and that there was enough food left over to fill twelve baskets.

There is so much one could say about this glorious example of a miracle of provision but the main point I want to make is that believers can again do the works of Jesus today, including miracles of provision. I have known food and even clothes items supernaturally being multiplied when believers have prayed in faith in situations of desperate need.

6. MIRACLES OF HEALING

These involve the dramatic, instant, total and public healing of a physical sickness or disability, leading to people marvelling at the greatness of God.

Jesus performed such miracles all the time in the two to three years of his public ministry, especially in Galilee. As he prayed, the blind began to see, the deaf hear and the lame leap for joy. In addition lepers were cleansed and the dead were raised. Whenever these things happened, they happened publicly and dramatically, evoking a sense of awe in those who witnessed these things.

I believe with all my heart that there are believers anointed and empowered to do the same works that Jesus did. I include in this 'creative healing miracles' – where we pray for new limbs and organs to be supernaturally given. We should long to see such things.

7. MIRACLES OF CONVERSION

I have left this until number 7 because in Jewish thought seven is the perfect number.

While I am always impressed by examples of the other six kinds of miracle, it is this one that still moves me most. Dramatic conversions are for me the perfect kind of miracle.

Always remember that Jesus not only healed and delivered people in his ministry, he also saved them from their sins. In his presence, sinners found forgiveness, mercy and kindness.

Those whom the religious people of his day condemned and rejected, Jesus welcomed and accepted. His meal tables were particularly powerful pictures in this regard; they were in effect banquets for the broken. As Jesus provided an environment of inclusion, people experienced transformation.

These miracles of transformation were every bit as profound as the miraculous transformation of water into wine. Truly, no one has ever had the power to change someone's life more quickly or more profoundly than Jesus of Nazareth.

He is truly the Wonderful Counsellor and the Prince of Peace. He is the friend of sinners, familiar with our sorrows. He brought peace to troubled hearts then, and he does the same today. He helped people from darkness to light then, and he does the same today. He forgave people totally then, and he does the same today.

The good news is that the Father wants to use us today to help people to come to the cross where they can receive salvation from their sins.

We are the adopted sons and daughters of the King of Heaven. We have the authority to do the works of Jesus today, including miracles such as these.

All it takes is a little faith.

So these are the seven kinds of miraculous works that we see in Jesus' ministry and indeed in churches which believe in miracles. We should not be surprised that these kinds of miracles are increasing throughout the world today, especially among charismatic and Pentecostal Christians. Jesus said to his disciples that they would do the same works as he had done and that they would do even greater works (John 14:12).

In John's Gospel the word 'works' refers to the miracles of Jesus – to turning water into wine, multiplying food, healing the sick and raising the dead.

Jesus tells his followers that in the future they will do greater works because he is going to the Father. In other words, he will no longer be localized in one place, in his physical body, healing those in physical proximity to him. Rather, from the right hand of the Father he will pour out the Holy Spirit on all those who confess his name.

Those who receive the Holy Spirit and who pray for miracles will see a far greater quantity and even quality of miraculous works. There will not be just one man in Galilee performing miracles; there will be countless men and women seeing signs and wonders globally.

If Jesus promised that we would do even greater works than he had done, why aren't some Christians seeing this?

....

....

....

....

....

....

What's going to be required of us if we are going to receive and use the gift of miraculous works?

I believe the following will be essential:

1. WE WILL NEED TO RENOUNCE THE NATURALIST MINDSET

The worldview that lies behind our secular age has been described as 'naturalism'. Naturalism is the belief that everything that we observe and experience in the world can be explained using the categories of natural law. There is therefore no need to resort to supernatural explanations for anything (supernaturalism). Everything we see and encounter can be understood using rational, materialistic categories; there is now no longer any room for talk about God, angels, demons or anything spiritual.

It stands to reason that if we are to even begin to use the gift of miraculous works we will need to renounce any allegiance we have to this demonic mindset. This is one of the strongholds that the enemy has had over people's minds for a long time in our secular culture. It is a mindset based on deception and lies. While no one in their right minds wants to undermine the achievements of science or the importance of reason, the truth is there is much in our world that the natural mind cannot understand.

The Apostle Paul put it this way in 1 Corinthians 2:14:

> *The person without the Spirit does not accept the things that come from the Spirit of God but considers them foolishness, and cannot understand them because they are discerned only through the Spirit.*

The natural mind cannot begin to understand the realities that come from the Holy Spirit.

Only the mind that is submitted to Jesus Christ and yielded to the Holy Spirit can discern these things.

In order to use the gift of miraculous works we may need to renounce the mindset of naturalism, one of the strongholds of our age. We may need to ask the Holy Spirit to release our minds from the stronghold of naturalism and to renew it with the mind of Christ – which is the mindset of the kingdom of heaven.

2. WE WILL NEED TO BELIEVE THAT MIRACLES ARE FOR TODAY

If we are to begin to use the gift of miraculous works there are two versions of Christian teaching that you will need to renounce. Both of these were forged in the so-called Age of Reason, also known as the Age of Enlightenment (from approximately 1789–1989). Both of these versions of the Christian faith are profoundly hostile to the working of miracles.

The first kind of Christianity is often referred to as 'liberal'. In the twentieth century, liberal Christianity was characterized by a deep scepticism concerning anything supernatural in the Holy Scriptures. Many liberal theologians attempted to strip all supernatural elements away from the Bible, believing that these had the character of myth rather than history.

With regard to miracles, the standard liberal position has been that miracles didn't happen then (in the Bible) and they don't happen now.

The second kind of Christianity is often referred to as 'conservative'. In the twentieth century, conservative Christianity was characterized by a deep scepticism concerning anything supernatural in contemporary Christian experience. Many conservative Christians tried to claim that healing and other miracles ceased at the end of the first century AD.

With regard to miracles, the standard conservative position has been that miracles did happen then (in the Bible) but that they don't happen now.

If we are going to operate in the gift of miraculous works we will need to turn away from both these faulty expressions of Christianity.

Both of these versions of Christianity were attempts to provide a rationalistic faith relevant to a rationalistic age. What was lost in both was a confident faith in the supernatural power of God. Both in the end have led to a powerless Christianity.

If we are to pray for and indeed see miracles (of whatever kind) we will need to believe that they happened in the Bible and that they happen today. We will need to turn away from cynicism (which says 'not then, not now') and cessationism (which says 'yes then, not now') and embrace 'continuationism' (which says 'yes then, yes now!').

3. WE WILL NEED TO EXERCISE AND GROW OUR FAITH IN GOD

If we are to begin to use and then excel in the gift of miraculous works we must learn to appreciate the importance of a living and active faith in God.

Faith in God is the doorway to the miraculous.

The Apostle Paul made this clear when he was challenging the believers in Galatia. He reminds them that it was faith in Christ that brought miracles into their lives.

In Galatians 3:5 he asks:

> *Does God give you his Spirit and work miracles among you by the works of the law, or by your believing what you heard?*

In other words, 'Does experience of the Holy Spirit – including miracles – come by obeying the law or by believing the gospel message?'

The answer for Paul is, 'By believing in Jesus, crucified and resurrected.'

Faith is accordingly the doorway to the miraculous.

What Paul is talking about here is 'conversion faith', the faith that saves us. If we are to see miracles, we must first receive our own miracle: the perfect miracle of conversion, which comes by repenting of sin and believing in Jesus.

But then there is 'continuing faith'. If we are going to see miracles, we will need to continue to exercise our faith, even when we see nothing. Even when there are apparently no answers to prayer, we will need to go on believing.

Then there is finally 'charismatic faith' or 'the gift of faith'. Notice that the gifts of healing and miraculous works come directly after the gift of faith in 1 Corinthians 12:1–11.

It seems to me that we will never break through into a dynamic ministry of working miracles without this third kind of faith. Like the other two kinds (conversion and continuing faith), charismatic faith is a gift from God. But this is not a licence to be passive; faith is like a muscle, it needs to be constantly exercised.

4. WE WILL NEED TO BE COMMITTED TO THE KINGDOM OF GOD

If we are to see miracles, then it's not just faith we need. We also need a deep desire to see the kingdom of God, because miracles are signs that Abba Father's royal presence has truly appeared among us.

There are at least two understandings of the kingdom of God.

In the first, it is argued that the kingdom of God (also known as the kingdom of heaven) started to invade in the first coming of Jesus but will only be fully established on the earth after his second coming. This view of the kingdom uses the words 'now and not yet'. The kingdom of heaven has already come (now) but is yet to come completely (not yet). We live in the tension between the now and the not yet of the kingdom.

Consequently, when we pray for miracles, sometimes we see the kingdom come now (the evidence being a dramatic answer to prayer). At other times we sense that the kingdom hasn't yet fully come (there is a sense of 'not yet').

In the second view, it is argued that the kingdom of God is the kingdom of heaven and when we pray 'Your kingdom come' we are praying for an invasion of heaven in the lives of those who are experiencing hell on earth. In this understanding, heaven is perfection. It is that spiritual realm where there is no cancer, no blindness, no deafness, no immobility, no sickness and no death. When heaven invades, these infirmities have to disappear.

Consequently, when we pray for heaven to invade, miracles should always occur. If they don't, the problem is not on God's side but on ours. If miracles aren't happening, it's because we haven't brought enough of heaven to earth.

In the first view, it's all a matter of time. The kingdom has partially come in the ministry of Jesus and will fully come at the end of time. In the meantime, miracles are a sign that the kingdom has come now.

In the second view, it's more a matter of space. The kingdom of heaven invades our earthly space when we pray in faith and when it does we see miracles. The more of heaven we have in our lives, the more miracles we will see.

Whichever of these two views you embrace, develop a deep desire to see the kingdom of God here on the earth.

5. WE WILL NEED TO LONG FOR SIGNS AND WONDERS

There is a view in Christian circles that we shouldn't be hungry to see signs, wonders and miracles today. The basis for this is Jesus' criticism of those that looked for miracles in his own day.

One example is found in the story of the royal official in John 4:43–54, who comes to Jesus with an entourage of attendants, pleading with Jesus to heal his little boy who is very sick back home. In John 4:48 Jesus responds:

'Unless you people see signs and wonders . . . you will never believe.'

Now it's really important to remember the context here if we are to understand fully what Jesus is saying. Remember that a text without a context can become a pretext – a pretext for just about any kind of wrong thinking.

The context here involves not only the father begging for his son but also a large retinue of onlookers who have travelled with him. He is there out of desperation. They are there out of curiosity.

It is not the father that Jesus is accordingly chastising when he says, 'Unless you people see a miracle you won't believe.' It is the group of people who have come in the hope of seeing a sensational supernatural spectacle. It is to these people that Jesus turns when he rounds on those whose faith in him is dependent on seeing him perform a miracle. It is to them that he addresses his rebuke, not the dad. Indeed, he grants the dad his request and heals his boy.

We should remember that it is certainly not wrong to want to see miracles if that desire is born of a deep desperation and compassion for a loved one or ones. Jesus would never condemn that. What Jesus condemns is the attitude that says, 'Unless I see miracles, I won't believe.'

So cultivate an intense hunger to see more miracles in your ministry and do this because of a relentless love for broken people.

Pray fervently like the earliest church did in Acts 4:30 for the Father to stretch out his hand to heal and perform signs and wonders.

Remember, the kingdom of heaven is for the desperate.

6. We Will Need to Cultivate a Childlike Spirit

One of the most important verses for accessing the realm of the miraculous is Matthew 18:3 where Jesus tells his disciples that unless they change and become like little children they will never enter the kingdom of heaven.

One of the things that I have noticed about friends of mine who see miracles on an ongoing basis is that they have what I would describe as a persistent and childlike love for the King and the kingdom. In other words, they have maintained over the long haul a beautiful naivety in their believing – a kind of childlike enthusiasm for Jesus and for his glory that has truly stood the test of time.

Right now I am thinking of a couple who travel the world speaking about Jesus to many thousands of people every year. They have not become fatigued or cynical, disappointed or frustrated. They are still full of childlike enthusiasm.

From time to time – like many of us – they have sometimes not seen what they longed to see. They haven't always seen blind eyes open and cancer healed. Yet they have not allowed this to deflate them.

These two saints continue to put their childlike trust in God. They have resolutely refused to feed their souls on what God has not done and have resiliently chosen to feed their souls instead on what he has done.

And here is a vital point. What do you do when you run into what looks like unanswered prayer? What do you do when you pray for someone to receive a miracle and they don't?

Those with a childlike trust confront the mystery head on and take the problem into the secret place of prayer. They come before their heavenly Abba and contend all the more in the area of their disappointment.

What we do with apparent failure is therefore vital. Those who become cynical cease to see miracles. Those who fight even harder for the breakthrough start seeing even greater things (John 1:50–51).

Fostering and sustaining a childlike spirit is therefore vital. If we want to enter and see the kingdom of heaven we will need to position ourselves before Abba Father as trusting children.

7. WE WILL NEED TO KEEP ON PERSEVERING

When the Apostle Paul wrote to the church in Corinth he reminded them that when he had visited them before he had revealed the true marks of an apostle by doing signs, wonders and miracles among them 'with all perseverance'.

Looking at this verse, many of us are apt to focus more on the language of power than the language of perseverance. Yet the truth is no one is going to excel in the gift of miraculous works until they learn to persevere in prayer.

One of the heroes of the faith who illustrated this consistently was the healing evangelist, Smith Wigglesworth. If ever there was a person who prayed with unfailing endurance, it was Smith. He would go well past the point where most of us would have given up in order to see a sick person healed or a dead person raised.

Let's take an example.

Smith was once called to pray for a young girl who was dying of consumption. It was ten o'clock at night. He told the girl's mother, sisters and brother to go to bed so that he could pray for the girl without distraction.

Reluctantly they went and Smith got praying. He seemed to be face to face with both death and the devil. He continued to believe that 'God can change the hardest situation and make you know that he is Almighty'.

Smith prayed and prayed but it seemed like the heavens were brass. Then he saw the girl actually die before his eyes. Smith decided that it was time to increase the strength of his prayers and began to fight. Later he wrote:

I looked at the window and at that moment the face of Jesus appeared. It seemed as though a million rays of light were coming from his face. As I looked at one who had just passed away, the colour came back to the face. She rolled over and fell asleep. In the morning she woke early, put on a dressing gown and walked to the piano. She started to play and to sing a wonderful song. The mother and the sister and the brother had all come down to listen. The Lord had undertaken. A miracle had been wrought.

Smith had prayed for more than five hours (till 3.30 a.m.) before the breakthrough came. He had been tempted to give up but decided instead to intensify his prayer effort. He truly persevered. Later he was to reflect on the gifts of healing and miraculous works:

> You must not think that these gifts will fall upon you like ripe cherries.
> There is a sense in which you have to pay the price for everything you get.

'You have to pay the price.' How many of us, I wonder, want to hear that. We love the idea of ministering in power. But paying the price? We love the idea as sons and daughters of sharing in Christ's glory. But sharing in his sufferings?

Once, during some powerful meetings in New Zealand (where thousands were miraculously saved and healed through his ministry), Smith went for a walk along the seashore with the host pastor of the event. The pastor asked Smith what the secret was of ministering in such an intense and effective level of miracle-working power. He was curious to know the answer so that he, too, could see miracles.

Smith replied that he was very sorry that the man had asked him this question but that he would answer. And this is what he said:

> I am a broken-hearted man. My wife who meant everything to me died eleven years ago. After the funeral I went back and lay on her grave. I wanted to die there. But God spoke to me and told me to rise up and come away. I told him if he would give me a double portion of the Spirit – my wife's and my own – I would go and preach the gospel. God was gracious to me and answered my request. But I sail the high seas alone. I am a lonely man, and many a time all I can do is to weep and weep.

Smith concluded that what he carried was not to be envied, but that he envied what the last generation of believers would carry. He had seen it in a vision and declared that it was unlike anything that had been seen in church history.

Smith Wigglesworth is an abiding reminder to all of us that we have to be prepared to persevere if we are going to see the power of God. We have to be prepared to pay a price if we are to see the prize.

The great men and women of God that I have met and known over the last twenty-five years have all had to pay a heavy price, especially those that have ministered in the gift of miraculous works. But they all would say that the breakthroughs made the battles worthwhile.

What do you need to work on most in your life if you are going to see more miracles when you pray?

....

....

....

....

....

....

The gift of miraculous works is given to some in the body of Christ. It is not given to everyone (see 1 Corinthians 12:27–30). But it is given to some.

Every local church needs to have members who are anointed and empowered to work miracles, not just within the church (during worship meetings) but outside the church on the streets.

One of the most exciting and encouraging things that's going on in the church today is the rediscovery of the gifts of healing and miraculous works in evangelism – in sharing the gospel with those who aren't Christians. Movements like Healing on the Streets (HOTS) are catching on in a massive way all over the UK, Europe and beyond. They are equipping believers to go into their towns and cities and pray for the sick to be healed outside the church.

The reports and testimonies that I'm hearing from all over are truly wonderful.

A few years ago I was preparing to speak in a Sunday morning service at a church in the UK. I had been invited for the whole weekend to minister at a conference there. Just before I spoke the pastor shared this testimony:

> Yesterday, Saturday morning, our Healing on the Streets team went out as usual and prayed for the sick in our city. They didn't have a large number of people respond to the invitation to receive prayer but one story did stand out for them.
>
> A Muslim man was walking past the banner with the word 'Healing' on it and the chairs when he turned round and asked, 'What are you lot into?'
>
> One of the team replied, 'We're into healing. Why do you ask?'
>
> The Muslim man replied that he had suffered from an acute back problem for a long time, accompanied by a high degree of pain. He then added, 'As I walked past you the pain went immediately and I know I'm healed.'
>
> With that, one of the team sat down with the man and explained that it was Jesus who had done this miracle. They then added, 'If Jesus did it, then that means Jesus is alive. And if Jesus is alive, then that means he's more than a prophet; he's the Son of God and you can know him today!'

How we need the gift of miraculous works today, not just inside the church when believers have great needs and trials, but outside the church as we share the gospel with lost people.

Isn't it time we prayed for this gift?

What am I going to do as a result of what I've learned in this chapter?

....

....

....

....

....

....

....

....

....

....

....

....

6

THE GIFT OF PROPHECY

To another is given the gift of prophecy.

1 Corinthians 12:10

> The gift of prophecy is the God-given ability to speak out revelation that has been suddenly brought to mind by the Holy Spirit.

I doubt if there are many things more encouraging than to be given a prophecy by someone who has no idea what's going on in your life but whose word reveals what only God could have known.

To be given a message by someone else that is both relevant and clearly Spirit-inspired is one of the most reassuring signs that Abba Father knows you by name and is personally interested in your life.

Indeed, receiving a striking prophetic word from another believer is like receiving a personally addressed letter from your Father in heaven. I can't think of many things more affirming than that.

Can you recall a time when you badly needed a word from God and someone gave you a prophecy that released hope into your heart?...

....

....

....

I remember a time when I was discouraged and felt like giving up. I was the senior leader of a flagship church but everything I tried to make the church grow had failed. In fact, we were actually losing people – including half the members of my staff team (about ten people in as many months).

Eventually this took its toll and I was signed off with burn-out. The tipping point came when I went for a weekend of rest to Iceland. I am not quite sure why I thought that a weekend on an island that resembles a lunar landscape would in any sense have been restful but perhaps this gives you an indication of the measure of my exhaustion and confusion.

When I returned I crashed. For more than three months I was too tired to do anything other than slowly get up in the morning, have a bath and climb onto the sofa in the sitting-room in my home. There I would stay until about 9 p.m. when I would start the process of going back upstairs to bed.

During this dark time, it seemed like everything was stripped away.

I didn't want to see anyone apart from my immediate family. I lost concentration whenever I tried to study the Bible. I got quickly tired and distracted when I tried to pray.

It was a wilderness to which I never want to return.

There were very few things that sustained me during this desert season, but the one thing I do remember making a big difference to me was a Scripture passage that I stumbled upon during one of my generally ineffective attempts to read the Bible and listen to God. It was a passage that became immediately luminous.

I am referring to Hebrews 10:35–37 (NLT):

Do not throw away this confident trust in the Lord. Remember the great reward it brings you! Patient endurance is what you need now, so that you will continue to do God's will. Then you will receive all that he has promised. 'For in just a little while, the Coming One will come and not delay.'

I don't know quite why I had never noticed this passage before but it felt like it had been written just for me. It was as if my heavenly Father was calling out to me, reminding me of the things I had been prepared to endure since I fell in love with his Son as a new Christian, urging me to keep pressing on because there were unfulfilled promises in my life – not least the promise of a visitation of the Holy Spirit. It was as if I heard him say, 'Persevere and press in . . . I'm coming soon.'

What happened next was a turning point. The following morning I received a 'get well' card from a friend whom I hadn't seen in a long while. In fact, the last time I had met her was at a day conference at my church. At that time she would have described herself as a non-charismatic Christian – someone who didn't believe that the gifts of the Spirit are available for believers today. At the end of one of the sessions I had told her the Father wanted her to receive the gift of prophecy because he had things he wanted her to share with others.

She told me afterwards that from that moment on she began to receive words of revelation for other people – even strangers – that brought encouragement to their lives.

The card I received from her during my burn-out was the first contact I'd had from her in a long time. All she knew was that I was off work suffering from exhaustion. When I opened it I found a handwritten message inside. She said she had sensed the Holy Spirit lay it upon her heart to share a Bible passage with me. When I read it I found it was exactly the same passage from Hebrews 10 that the Father had given me the day before.

Within a few days I was back at work.

Within a few years, we saw the beginning of what was a wonderful move of the Holy Spirit – a move Andrew Williams and I describe in the book *Breakout*.

Don't you just love it when God speaks to you like this through the Scriptures?

> **Have you ever been struck by a verse or verses which another believer subsequently shared as a word for you?**
>
> ....
> ....
> ....
> ....
> ....

This chapter is all about the gift of prophecy – which I have defined as 'the God-given ability to speak out revelation that has been suddenly brought to mind by the Holy Spirit'.

What are the ways in which prophetic revelation comes to us?

THE FATHER SPEAKS TO US THROUGH SCRIPTURE

Sometimes a Scripture passage will suddenly come to mind that you are to share with another person. When you give it to them, you often find that this is a passage which God has put on their hearts too. And this can be an immensely encouraging experience.

Right now I'm thinking of a time a few years ago when I was sitting on the deck of a lovely house in a forest in the State of Ohio in the USA. I was having a barbecue with the owner of the house – the pastor of a church at which I was speaking during those days.

As I looked at him I sensed the Holy Spirit bringing words from the very last verse of the book of Jonah to mind – words spoken by God to the prophet:

'Should I not have compassion on Nineveh, the great city?'

(Jonah 4:11, NASB)

When a suitable moment presented itself I shared the verse with him. He was visibly moved. He told those of us present that the previous week he had been sitting on a park bench in a downtown, run-down part of the city. As he sat there an old dog came and sat beside him. As he looked at the stray animal he felt sorry for it and started stroking it. As he did he sensed the Father saying to him, 'You know, my son, you have more compassion for this lonely dog than you do for all the broken people in this city.'

As soon as he heard that, the pastor began to repent and, as he did, the Spirit of God spoke the following words into his heart: 'Should I not have compassion on . . . this great city?'

When I gave him exactly the same verse it was a confirmation to him that he was being called to start a compassion ministry in a deprived part of the city – an area that his church was not reaching.

The next time I visited him several years later he drove me to a disused church property that his congregation had recently purchased and were turning into a resource designed to serve the inner-city community.

So the Father speaks to us through his book, the Bible. The Bible contains the highest, purest kind of revelation. No prophetic vision or dream, word or message, has the same level of authority as the Bible. Anyone who claims that their revelation is greater than the revelation given to the biblical writers is not to be trusted. God's written revelation eclipses all other kinds of revelation in terms of reliability, permanency and authority.

I want to encourage you to be open to the Holy Spirit giving you a passage of Scripture for someone else. You never know, it could launch a powerful ministry to the poor, or revive a weary and discouraged pastor.

Is there a passage of Scripture that the Father is impressing on you right now to share with another person?

....

....

....

....

....

....

THE FATHER SPEAKS TO US THROUGH DREAMS

I don't know whether you are conscious of having dreams. Most of my dreams are very strange and not at all memorable – more the product of late night cheese than supernatural revelation. But just occasionally I have a striking dream which I just know is from the Father and which I need to interpret and apply in my life.

I remember one time having a vivid and disturbing dream of me trying to reverse out of my driveway in my car and running into my children. I was utterly traumatized by this experience and woke up in a cold sweat. I asked the Lord what it meant and as soon as I did I got the distinct impression that this was a warning dream and that it was not about my own children but about children in the community. I sensed that children were in danger and that I was to pray. I don't remember spending a long time interceding after that, maybe a couple of minutes during my morning devotional time. But I do remember being fervent, because the dream had been so vivid and had so deeply affected me emotionally that I had no choice but to pray in a passionate way.

That very afternoon someone told me that a car had been parked on a hill near the school gates. The handbrake had failed and the car had started to roll backwards. Two school children had been directly in the path of the car and looked like they were going to be run over but at the last moment the vehicle had veered away from them and lodged itself in a large hedge in front of a neighbour's front garden. Everyone who saw it was amazed that the children had not been hurt, or worse.

As I heard this report I was deeply grateful. I just knew that my dream had been a call to prayer and that my brief prayers had been heard and answered.

Even more encouraging was the fact that these two girls were daughters of a woman who was not a Christian but to whom some of us had been witnessing for months. She lived in an area of our community which we were trying to reach and she worked in a restaurant I went to from time to time.

The next time I went there for a meal I was able to take her on one side and tell her about the dream and about my prayers. That moved her deeply and drew her closer to Jesus and got her asking about church.

Be attentive to your dreams.

God has often spoken to his people through them.

While there are many different kinds of dream (see the following list), one of the most common is the kind illustrated by my testimony – the warning dream. We should not be surprised if our Father speaks to us in this way. As Job 33:15–16 says in The Message:

In a dream, for instance, a vision at night, when men and women are deep in sleep, fast asleep in their beds – God opens their ears and impresses them with warnings.

DIFFERENT KINDS OF PROPHETIC DREAMS

1. Calling Dreams
Dreams that reveal part of our God-given destiny and release a new sense of purpose.

2. Comforting Dreams
Dreams that bring healing, often through helping us to see the past from a new perspective.

3. Courage Dreams
Dreams that encourage us to take an urgent course of action.

4. Correctional Dreams
Dreams that reveal issues of our hearts and which invite repentance.

5. Cleansing Dreams
Dreams which usually involve being drenched in water and which symbolize purification.

6. Cautionary Dreams
Dreams that warn us about something destructive and which invite us to intercede.

7. Creative Dreams
Dreams that give us new insights, ideas, images, designs, songs, stories, titles and so on.

8. Course-Setting Dreams
Dreams that give specific guidance about the direction we need to take.

9. Clarifying Dreams
Dreams that teach and instruct you, bringing clarity at a crucial time.

10. Call-to-Arms Dreams
Dreams that give insight into the spiritual battle and also faith for the victory.

Note:
This list is not exhaustive and the dreams above often overlap

Go through this list now, then consider the following question:

Have you ever had a dream which you thought was prophetic?

....

....

....

....

....

....

....

I want to encourage you to be open to the Holy Spirit giving you prophetic dreams. When you do, remember that some are meant to be shared and some are meant to be turned into intercessory prayer. Either way, they will be 'for the common good'.

The Father Speaks to Us Through Visions

In my experience there are two kinds of vision.

Closed visions

These are usually presented to the waking mind in a sequence of images and words as on a movie screen.

One example is in Acts 18. Here Paul is speaking in Corinth and clearly thinking of moving on to a different city. He had been harshly opposed by some of his fellow Jews and he was experiencing intimidation, so he was considering leaving the city. At this point the Father speaks (Acts 18:9–11):

> *One night the Lord spoke to Paul in a vision: 'Do not be afraid; keep on speaking, do not be silent. For I am with you, and no one is going to attack*

and harm you, because I have many people in this city.' So Paul stayed in
Corinth for a year and a half, teaching them the word of God.

In this vision, Paul was simply told what to do. He was not invited to
speak or to act, just to hear and obey. He was given an encouraging
and comforting message which strengthened his resolve to such a
degree that he stayed another eighteen months in Corinth and taught
the people without fear.

Many visions given to believers today are of this kind. They are
visions in which we watch and listen to what the Father is doing and
saying. They are 'closed' like a film is 'closed'. In other words, you
are simply watching and listening not speaking or acting within the
vision.

Open visions

Open visions are different from closed visions in that they elicit
the involvement of the one who receives them. In other words, the
one seeing the vision actually gets to participate in the drama that's
unfolding in the vision. Unlike closed visions, they get to speak and
sometimes act in it.

One of the best examples of an open vision in the Bible is the
one given to Ezekiel about a valley of dry bones. In Ezekiel 37, the
Spirit of God takes the prophet to a vast plain where there are many
dried-up bones, bleached by the intense heat of the sun. God speaks
to Ezekiel and asks him if the dry bones can now live. Ezekiel replies
that only God knows.

At this point God tells Ezekiel to proclaim the word of the Lord
that they will live. As the prophet then makes his decree the bones
join together to form human skeletons covered in muscle, sinew, liga-
ments and flesh.

A second phase of the vision now begins. God tells Ezekiel to
prophesy to the breath from the four corners of the earth. The prophet

obeys and watches as the breath of God fills the lifeless bodies which become an army of living people. These bodies are then filled as well as formed.

This is clearly an open vision because the one seeing it plays a significant part in what takes place. In other words, Ezekiel is not a passive spectator; he is an active participator. Without his declaration, the bones would have remained lifeless in the valley. He needed to speak if they were going to live.

Sometimes the Father speaks to his sons and daughters through open visions – even today. In these kinds of visions we are invited to co-operate with the Holy Spirit in activating the Father's purposes for his people.

How we need the Father to mobilize a living army today – formed for innovative mission and filled with the flame of his love.

Have you ever had a 'closed' or 'open' vision?

....

....

....

....

....

....

....

God's Word clearly teaches us that Abba Father gives dreams and visions to his children from the day of Pentecost onwards. As far as the earliest Christians were concerned, the coming of the Holy Spirit marked the beginning of the last days of history. These days would be characterized by an unusual, indeed unprecedented, release of the gift of prophecy in the lives of God's people. As Peter proclaims in Acts 2:17:

'In the last days,' God says, 'I will pour out my Spirit on all people. Your sons and daughters will prophesy, your young men will see visions, your old men will dream dreams.'

Notice here how generations and genders are included in this promise. Believers of all ages and both sexes will start to prophesy after the outpouring of the Spirit at Pentecost. As far as our heavenly Father is concerned, the church is called to be a prophetic family.

Notice also how this passage shows how prophecy has to be distinguished from preaching. Some mistakenly view prophecy and preaching as the same. But this verse shows that prophecy involves seeing visions and dreaming dreams. That is hardly the same thing as preaching, although people have been known to start dreaming when others have been preaching!

So the Bible clearly teaches that we are to expect to receive revelation through visions and dreams.

And the experience of those who are open to the gift of prophecy only serves to prove the point.

I have already given an example of a prophetic dream from my own story. Now let me share about a vision.

In my early twenties my life could have gone in a number of directions. I was a first-year undergraduate at Cambridge University and I think it's fair to say that I was being tempted to pursue dreams that were not God's 'Plan A' for my life.

At the end of my first term I returned to my parents' house and went to bed the first night of the holidays feeling tired but happy to be home. I fell into a deep sleep almost immediately. Within what seemed like a few moments I woke with a start, looking at my digital alarm clock. It read '1:06' in a bright, glowing, green light.

As I looked at the clock wondering why I was awake, my bedroom door flew open. I had shut it – as I always did – to keep my mother's cat out of my room. I wasn't fond of it and it had the nasty habit of lying on my chest when I was asleep.

When the door swung open, I saw something that utterly arrested me.

There, standing in front of me, was a bright figure, at least six feet tall. There was an extraordinary amount of light radiating from every part of his body. As I looked up, the light in and around his face was so brilliant that I was unable to make out any definite features. I was just aware of a face as bright as the sun.

I knew it was Jesus.

Then the figure reached out his hand and beckoned to me.

As he did so I just heard the words 'follow me' – not audibly but as an unmistakable impression in my spirit.

As I heard, I obeyed. All I remember was saying the word 'yes' over and over.

Then I fell asleep.

When I woke up the next morning I rushed into my parents' bedroom and told them what had happened. The extraordinary thing was that they immediately believed me.

Clearly I was carrying something supernatural from the encounter – maybe a kind of afterglow that increased the credibility of my testimony. Whatever the reason, my father and mother accepted what I said. From that day on I set the wheels in motion to explore a calling to full-time ordained ministry with my local bishop. Within five years I was starting my ministry as a pastor. All because I had received an open vision in the night in which Jesus had asked me to follow him, and I had said 'yes'.

Have you ever had a vision in which God called you to change direction in your life?

....

....

....

....

....

....

In this chapter I have been describing how God's adopted sons and daughters can prophesy today. The gift of prophecy is not a deluxe gift given only to a super-spiritual group in the church. It is a present that the Father wants all of his children to open. It is for every believer.

So far I have been mainly focusing on what we might call the more 'visual' kinds of revelation. In dreams and visions, the Father speaks to us in striking pictures. These are often symbolic in nature and require us to go through a prayerful process of interpreting and then applying what we have seen.

As has been said many times by many others, when it comes to dreams and visions the Father challenges us to go through a threefold process involving:

This is important. Visual prophecy tends to be highly metaphorical. Verbal prophecy, on the other hand, tends to be more obvious in its meaning. Put another way, dreams and visions can be quite surreal and enigmatic. Direct messages are more normally quite easy to comprehend.

Thus, with the dream about my children being run over, I could have gone into a panic and thought that God was warning me about my driving. While that would have been entirely appropriate, it wasn't what God was trying to say. He used the picture of my own children to evoke a deep desire to pray for children in my parish. Later that day I understood what the dream had really meant.

Sometimes it really is the glory of God to conceal a matter. He tests our resolve to understand him. While at times we may plead like the disciples did for Jesus to speak plainly to us, not in mysterious word-pictures, a lot of the time he wants us to search out the meaning of what we see.

It is our pursuit that pleases him.

THE FATHER SPEAKS TO US THROUGH WORDS

What this indicates is that there are other ways in which the Father speaks to us prophetically – ways which are less visual and pictorial than what we receive in dreams and visions.

To back this up, let me just remind you of the story of Zerubbabel in the Old Testament. He was called by God to lead 50,000 Jewish exiles back from Babylon to their home city of Jerusalem in 538 BC. His assignment was to rebuild the temple which had been sacked by the Babylonians in 587 BC.

Zerubbabel started the building project but it ground to a halt two years later because the people were grumbling that what they were building was not going to be as glorious as the temple that their forefathers had built.

I wonder if you've ever heard that before!

For sixteen years Zerubbabel couldn't motivate the people to get to work again and he was deeply discouraged. Then in 520 BC God raised up two prophets to rally him.

The first was called Zechariah. He was a man who received very visual, symbolic, pictorial revelations. If you read the book of Zechariah you'll quickly appreciate that Zechariah was a 'seer' – someone who saw things through supernatural and revelatory spectacles. His prophecies often came in the form of night visions and were strange to say the least. So, for example, in one of his visions he sees a man on a red horse, in another four horns and four craftsmen, in another a man with a measuring line, in another a flying scroll and in another (my personal favourite) a woman sitting in a basket!

It is therefore fair to say that Zechariah received revelation mostly in the form of symbolic visions that required interpretation before they could be applied.

The other prophet whom God raised up was called Haggai. His prophecies are recorded in the very short Old Testament book by the same name (only two chapters in length).

Haggai's prophecies were very different from Zechariah's. If Zechariah's came in the form of God-pictures, Haggai's came in the form of God-thoughts. In other words, Haggai's prophecies are far less visual than Zechariah's. Haggai receives verbal prophecies like, 'Give careful thought to your ways.' These words are messages from the Father heart of God that require little interpretation.

When Zerubbabel needed to be brought out of his discouragement, the Father raised up two prophets, one who spoke in a very indirect way (through arresting pictures) and one who spoke in a very direct way (through striking messages).

I am happy to report that these two prophets succeeded in encouraging Zerubbabel and the people to start building again and within four years the temple had been rebuilt and the people were gasping with gratitude.

Have you ever received a message from the Lord which was cast more in the form of a thought than a picture?

....

....

....

....

....

....

The story of Zerubbabel isn't just an interesting history lesson. It's also a fascinating pointer to the different ways in which the Father speaks to us. Broadly speaking there are two main ways, and I call these the Zechariah-type prophecy and the Haggai-type prophecy:

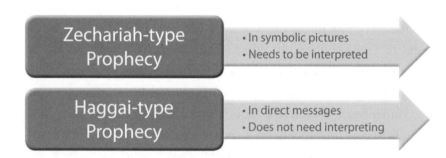

Zechariah-type Prophecy
• In symbolic pictures
• Needs to be interpreted

Haggai-type Prophecy
• In direct messages
• Does not need interpreting

When Zechariah prophesies to Zerubbabel he shares a night vision in which he sees Zerubbabel as an olive tree connected to an oil-filled, golden menorah or lampstand (Zechariah 4:2–3).

This certainly requires interpretation.

And the interpretation is that Zerubbabel is connected to the Father's oil supply – the Holy Spirit – and that with the help of the Spirit, not in his own strength, the building project will be completed (Zechariah 4:6).

That's the application.

Now let's see how Haggai's approach differs.

When Haggai prophesies to Zerubbabel, he simply says, '*I am with you*' (Haggai 1:13).

In a sense this is the same prophetic word. Zechariah had told Zerubbabel that he was connected to the oil of God's Spirit. That's another way of saying that God hadn't left and that he was right there with him. But Haggai goes directly to the point. He doesn't use symbolic pictures that require interpretation. He just looks at the embattled and depressed leader and says, '"*I am with you," says the Lord*'!

This should highlight for us that there is a variety of ways in which the Father speaks prophetically – one demonstrated by Zechariah and the other by Haggai.

Is one kind of prophetic revelation superior to another?

Not at all! A lot of this has to do with the way our brains function. Some of us are analytical and rational. Others are more artistic and mystical. I suspect that those who are used to operating out of the left side of the brain (the logical side) are more prone to receiving the Haggai-type prophecy. Those who live out of the right side of the brain (the artistic side) are probably more prone to receiving the Zechariah-type prophecy.

When the Father speaks, we therefore need to be open to the non-visual as well as the visual kinds of revelation.

We mustn't restrict prophecy to dreams and visions. We need to be open to receiving Haggai-type prophecies – direct messages from the Father-heart of God, messages like '*The glory of this present house will be greater than the glory of the former house*' (Haggai 2:9).

> **Have you ever received a message from the Lord which you are to give to someone else?**
>
> ....
> ....
> ....
> ....
> ....
> ....

At this point it might be helpful to give a modern-day example of a prophecy in the form of a message rather than a picture.

Not long ago I arrived at a hotel before speaking at a conference. I was earlier than I'd expected so I went to the foyer and sat at a coffee bar. I was the only customer so I got chatting to the young man serving me. His name was Mark. He asked me what I was doing in the area, so I explained that I was a preacher. His reaction to this was fascinating. He said, 'Oh that's interesting; my mum is a clairvoyant.' Clearly preachers and psychics were all part of the same tribe in his unsaved mind! He then added, 'My mum can read other people really accurately.' I responded to that by saying, 'I know someone who can read other people's hearts more accurately than anyone else and his Spirit lives within me, and his Spirit helps me to read other people's hearts.'

You know when sometimes you say something before you have fully engaged your brain? That was me at that moment. I hadn't really thought about what I was saying, or what I was getting myself into by saying it, but the moment it was out there I knew what he would say next.

'Prove it.'

When you are in this kind of situation let me teach you a prayer that is absolutely indispensable. It is a foolproof prayer with extraordinary power. Are you ready to be enriched by my extraordinary theology?

Here it is.

The prayer you need in this situation is the four letter word: 'Help!'

That silent prayer had barely wended its way from my heart when some information came into my head suddenly and from out of left field.

I spoke out what I had received: 'I sense that your parents divorced ten years ago and that you have been so deeply affected by this that you cannot relate properly to your girlfriend because you are frightened of commitment.'

As soon as I said that, Mark's jaw dropped and his mouth opened wide.

He paused and then said, 'Wow!'

He went on to explain that his dad and mum had divorced exactly ten years before and that he had split up with his girlfriend the week before because he was afraid of experiencing what his parents had gone through.

He then added this amazing and memorable statement: 'Jesus is even more accurate than my mum!'

What followed after that was very moving. Mark shared how he was doing extra work at the coffee bar because his dad had moved to California and he wanted to earn enough money to go and live with him. He clearly missed his father dreadfully and was desperate to be with him.

I then used this open door of opportunity to talk to him about the one whom Jesus came to reveal – the Father who loves us like no earthly father ever could. I told him about my book, *The Father You've Been Waiting For* (Authentic, 2005), written specifically for those who aren't

Christians, and gave him a copy as a gift. And so, through prophecy, a spiritual orphan was brought closer to the world's greatest Dad.

What this testimony shows us is that revelation comes to us not just in pictures but also in messages – in direct statements about people or situations in the form of intuitions or hunches. These usually provide knowledge that only God could have given us – supernatural insights that lead others to recognize that God knows all about them and cares about their destiny as well as their history.

What is interesting about the story I've just told is the fact that the Father can give us messages for non-Christians as well as Christians. He can give us words for spiritual orphans as well as for his adopted sons and daughters. Prophecy can accordingly be used in evangelism – in speaking to non-Christians about Jesus – and not just in the church.

This emphasis on using the gift of prophecy in witnessing to others has been gaining momentum ever since my book *Prophetic Evangelism* (Authentic, 2004).

Let's not restrict the use of gifts like prophecy in witnessing and healing to Christian meetings. They are meant to be used outside the church too.

Have you ever had the opportunity to share a prophetic word with an unbeliever?

....

....

....

....

....

....

Intimacy and Insight

One final word about the gift of prophecy and that is this: the greater your intimacy, the greater your prophecy. The closer you lean on the heart of your Father, the clearer you will hear the voice of your Father.

If we want to excel in the gift of prophecy then we must learn first to excel in the art of intimacy.

No one ever prophesied with greater authority or accuracy than Jesus. But then no one in history has ever been as close to the Father's heart as Jesus was and is. And herein is a vital key for growing in the gift of prophecy. We need to become more like Jesus, the Son of God. Jesus is the Son of God by nature, and of him alone can this be said. But we are sons and daughters of God by adoption. Like Jesus, we are called to have such an intimate communion with Abba Father that we know the intonations of his voice and the beating of his heart.

In a healthy family, sons and daughters have a unique relationship with their father. While everyone else in that father's world may have a formal relationship, sons and daughters know him as 'Dad'. They hear him speak to them in a different tone from the one he uses with others.

In John 15:15 Jesus tells his disciples that he no longer calls them servants but friends. He then adds, *'because a servant does not know his master's business'*. Jesus then tells them that everything he's heard from the Father he's made known to them. In other words, they are now becoming friends of Jesus and sons of the Father. They now know things they didn't know before!

If you and I want to grow in the prophetic we need to enter into the fullness of what it means to be a son or a daughter. Slaves and servants know God as Master and have no access to his plans. Sons and daughters know God as Daddy and hear what he's thinking and saying. Revelation accordingly comes out of relationship.

There is therefore something far more fundamental that needs to be attended to if we are to receive and cultivate the gift of prophecy. This has to do with our relationship with God. The choice is ours: we can be slaves or we can be sons. God can be a distant Master or an affectionate Father. We can be deaf to his voice or we can learn to hear it clearly. The spirit of prophecy cannot be separated from the spirit of sonship.

What word best describes your relationship with God right now – slavery or sonship?

....

....

....

....

....

....

In the final analysis, we are encouraged to '*eagerly desire gifts of the Spirit, especially prophecy*' (1 Corinthians 14:1). In other words, we are urged to be hungry for the gift of prophecy. But all this needs to be put in context. The words preceding this say '*follow the way of love*'. The more you love the Father, the more you will hear the Father. And the more you love people, the more you will hear his heart for them.

So love the Giver more than you love the gift.

All this is to underline the truth that there is a vital connection between growing as a son or a daughter and growing in the prophetic.

Paul said that those who are the children of God are led by the Spirit of God (Romans 8:14). In other words, being led by the Spirit (which means living a prophetic lifestyle) is one of the infallible signs that we are sons and daughters as opposed to slaves and orphans. Good sons and daughters are good listeners. The adopted sons and daughters of God hear the Father's voice.

STEWARDING THE PROPHETIC

This makes a massive difference in the way that prophecy is handled. The more you live like an orphan or a slave, the more you will be prone to abusing the prophetic.

- Orphans use prophecy to manipulate people
- They don't submit to authority
- They do not prefer others in love
- They are destructive rather than constructive
- They inspire fear rather than comfort
- They are harsh rather than loving
- They behave with immaturity rather than maturity

Sons and daughters are the opposite.

- Sons and daughters use prophecy to release people
- They happily submit to loving authority
- They love hearing other people's voices more than their own
- They give words that build people up, not tear them down
- They leave people feeling comforted and affirmed by the Father
- They are gentle rather than aggressive
- They are committed to maturity

The Bible verse which best sums up how sons and daughters approach prophecy is Jeremiah 15:19. In the NASB it reads as follows:

If you extract the precious from the worthless, you will become my spokesman.

It seems to me that this is at the very heart of what it means to operate in the gift of prophecy. If we want to be God's spokesmen or spokeswomen, then we will need to learn to see what the Father sees when we look at other people and situations. Our Father could focus on what is worthless and broadcast that. But he looks at people with eyes that are shiny with outrageous kindness and sees instead the precious – and that is what he exposes and parades.

So there's a choice. When we look at others, we can say, 'When I look at you I see the trash.' Or we can look at others and say, 'When I look at you I see the treasure.'

In my experience, Christians with orphan hearts focus on the trash in other people's lives. Christians filled with the spirit of sonship focus on the treasure.

In the final analysis, that is the difference between religion and reality.

What am I going to do as a result of what I've learned in this chapter?

....

....

....

....

....

....

....

....

....

....

7

THE GIFT OF DISCERNMENT

To another is given gifts of discernment.

1 Corinthians 12:10

> The gift of discernment is the God-given ability to discern
> what is from the Holy Spirit and what is not.

Presents are strange things. I remember when I was a child my father had noticed that I was keenly interested in the Napoleonic wars. I had hand-painted a huge set of British and French toy soldiers with my mother and produced a re-enactment of the Battle of Waterloo which had covered most of my bedroom floor. I simply couldn't get enough of all things Napoleonic. I devoured history books about that era and I was in heaven when the movie *Waterloo* came out with Rod Steiger as Napoleon and Sir Christopher Plummer as the Duke of Wellington.

Noticing this, my father went on the hunt for a gift that fuelled that interest. Christmas was approaching and he was keen that my brother, sister and I received the best possible presents. I had set my heart on the latest popular toy. As I recall, it was a plastic horse-racing circuit which you plugged into the wall. Using joysticks, my sister and I planned to race our gaudy-coloured nags around the track in the days after Christmas.

When Christmas Day came it was time to unwrap the presents. I looked at mine while it was still in its paper and thought for a moment that something was wrong. It didn't seem to be the right size and dimensions for the track and horses. Something was not quite right and my small, snotty nose was now out of joint.

Sure enough, on tearing the paper, I discovered to my horror that my father had bought me the wrong present.

There, in place of the latest sought-after Christmas toy for boys, was a gilt-framed painting featuring Napoleonic cavalrymen in ceremonial uniform sitting on caparisoned horses.

I clearly registered my disapproval. Knowing me, I had a bit of a strop and probably asked why I had a painting of horses instead of ones that ran around a track.

I could tell my father was disappointed.

I had no idea of the trouble he took to find and buy my present. It didn't even occur to me that he might have engaged in an epic quest to find it.

My hard little heart was not to be moved and my stubborn little feet were stomping. My mother rightly tore a strip off me and told me I was ungrateful and to take the picture up to my room.

The next day my father came home with the race track and horses, handing them to me with a knowing smile.

The day after, in a particularly aggressive race with my twin sister Claire, the horse track broke irreparably and the present was from that day on completely unusable.

Today, of course, the horses and the track have long since disappeared – dissolved into the dust of the earth, never to be resurrected. The military painting, on the other hand, is one of my most prized possessions.

And nearly fifty years on, I'm writing a series of novels based in the Napoleonic era. My father clearly knew more about gift-giving than I did.

I share this anecdote because there are good spiritual gifts that we can take completely for granted. We underestimate their value and significance. We think they are lesser gifts than the more gaudy ones we'd prefer. In this, as in so many things, we are mistaken. We take the short-term and superficial view. Our Father, on the other hand, looks at the bigger picture, if you'll pardon the pun.

When we come to the spiritual gift of discernment, we are very likely to respond in the way I did to the painting. We think, 'Actually, I'd rather have one of the more dramatic power gifts – like miracles or healing. Discernment isn't the most attractive present. Father, give me something a bit more exciting.'

How wrong we can be!

The gift of discernment is, as we will now learn, one of the most important gifts of the Holy Spirit. It may seem at first sight to be a little disappointing when we realize we have been given it. But time is a great teacher and later on, when we are wiser and more mature, we recognize that this gift has not only shaped us but shaped those around us too.

Have you ever thought of your gift or gifts as less important and powerful than those given to others?

....

....

....

....

....

....

So what is 'the gift of discernment?' I define it as 'the God-given ability to discern what is from the Holy Spirit and what is not'.

The gift of discernment is one of the most marginalized and yet one of the most vital gifts for the body of Christ. We undervalue it to our great peril.

In the church today it would be safe to say that the gift and the ministry of prophecy have been given a great deal of airtime in books and conferences.

The same has not been true of the gift of discernment.

The Apostle Paul would have found this most bizarre. The gift of discernment is, after all, a companion to the gift of prophecy. Paul understood very well that prophecy and discernment were always meant to hang out together.

If the prophetic gift is like the ears of the body of Christ (the church), the gift of discernment is like the nose. The ears are sensitive to the supernatural voice of God. The nose sniffs out the pure from the impure.

Their synergy has to be respected at all times.

This is because the gift of discernment distinguishes between what is good – and worth holding on to – and what is bad – and therefore to be rejected.

When it comes to prophetic revelation, those gifted with discernment recognize what is from the Holy Spirit and what is not. It would have been inconceivable to Paul not to revere and use this gift. Such neglect would in his mind lead to many people spouting any kind of nonsense in the name of prophecy and the church gullibly believing it. For Paul, discernment was a *sine qua non* for the Spirit-filled church.

So what exactly did Paul mean by the gift of 'distinguishing between spirits', to use the actual phrase used in the NIV translation.

In the original Greek language the word translated 'discernment' denotes a process of thorough *evaluation*. It refers to a process of judging thoroughly and comprehensively.

In a sense, every member of the church is supposed to be a discerning Christian. When we receive a prophetic word ourselves, or from someone else, we are meant to subject these words to a battery of tests. We are not to assume or presume that they are 100 per cent from God. In fact, we should start with the assumption that the prophecy is only part of the picture, not the whole if it. No one ever hears the Father with complete accuracy. The only person who has ever lived who's done that was Jesus. What Jesus saw his Father doing he saw infallibly. What he heard from the Father he heard clearly and flawlessly. When Jesus spoke prophetically it was accordingly with absolute authority, absolute accuracy and absolute authenticity. No one else in history can claim that. No one else in history should claim that.

If you ever hear anyone saying that they hear God with unhindered and complete certainty, be very wary of them. Put clear blue water between yourself and them. The only person whose prophecies do not need to be tested are those that Jesus uttered and which are recorded in the New Testament. As the Son of God, by nature he had immediate and unobstructed access to the Father's heart and the Father's voice.

This is not true for us: every adopted son or daughter of God must put their prophetic words to the test. In short, we must exercise discernment.

If you are part of a church where prophecies are delivered but never evaluated, this needs to be rectified. The gift of discernment needs to be revered by everyone.

In your experience, to what extent are prophetic words subjected to a serious process of testing?

....

....

....

....

....

As we begin to unwrap this particular present, it is really important to understand what it is that we are called to discern. When someone delivers a prophecy, we are not meant to ask how poetic their language is, nor how striking their visuals are, but rather something much deeper than these outward expressions. We are called and tasked to ask where they come from.

Here the original language is helpful again. Paul says that the gift of discernment is the ability to distinguish between 'spirits'.

What, then, did he mean by 'spirits'?

There are basically three ways in which the word 'spirit' is used in the New Testament:

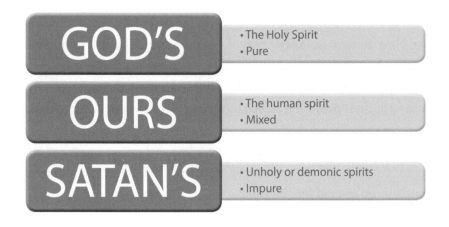

GOD'S
- The Holy Spirit
- Pure

OURS
- The human spirit
- Mixed

SATAN'S
- Unholy or demonic spirits
- Impure

1. THE HOLY SPIRIT

The first way in which the word spirit is used (*pneuma* in Greek) is with a capital 'S', referring to the Spirit of God (see 1 Corinthians 2:10).

Prophetic words can indeed come from the Holy Spirit. They can be motivated and inspired by the Spirit of God who is pure, trustworthy and comforting. When we are given a genuine prophecy, the Spirit behind it is the Holy Spirit.

2. THE HUMAN SPIRIT

The second way in which the word spirit is used is with a small 's'. Here 'spirit' refers to the spirit of a human being.

Sometimes it can be a little confusing when we read the New Testament because certain passages use the word *pneuma* or spirit to refer to the Holy Spirit in one instance and the human spirit in another. In Romans 8:16, for example, Paul talks about how the Holy Spirit testifies to our spirits that we are the children of God. Here the same word is used twice in the same sentence but in one case it refers to the Divine Spirit (the Third Person of the Trinity) whereas in the second instance it refers to the human spirit.

What then did Paul mean by the spirit in this more human sense?

According to the Scriptures, every human being has a spirit. This is the part of our humanity which is created by God to commune with him. Before we are born again, this spirit is dead because of sin. Sin separates us from God. Disconnected from the One who is the source of life, our spirits are dead. But once we come to Christ and through the Spirit of God are born again, then our human spirits become quickened and alive. The life of the Holy Spirit floods the deep reservoirs of our human spirits so that we can know that God is our Father and we are his beloved children.

Let's stay on this thought a little longer.

Up until the time we come to Christ and receive salvation, our human nature is corrupted by sin. Put another way, the operating system within us is faulty and unstable. When we choose to follow Christ, however, that system is restored to its factory settings. It is realigned to the Creator's original design. Does this mean that this rebooted system is no longer vulnerable to viruses? Not at all, this spirit has been restored but it has not yet been perfected. It is not immune from the viruses of error and deception.

This has implications for the discernment of prophetic revelation.

Whenever a person gifted with discernment hears a prophecy, they are mandated by God to assess whether that utterance comes from the pure and undiluted source which is the Holy Spirit or from the restored but still fallible human spirit. In short they are called to ask whether this is a word from heaven or just a word of their own.

Sometimes, in a genuine desire to comfort another person or a group of people, we may fall into the trap of prophesying out of our own heart and strength rather than with the mind of Christ. When this happens we must be prepared to be real about it and, where necessary, to apologize humbly, admitting that we have prophesied out of our own spirit rather than the Holy Spirit.

3. DEMONIC SPIRITS

There is a third possible source for words that can sometimes appear prophetic and this is demonic or unholy spirits. Demonic spirits are spirits that create close and sometimes compelling counterfeits to true revelation. It is perhaps for this reason more than any other that we need the gift of discernment, the gift of distinguishing spirits.

The Gospels clearly describe the existence of evil and destructive spirits. Jesus confronted them all the time in his ministry. Every time he did, he cast them out of the person being tormented by them.

Belief in such evil spirits may seem to be the last vestiges of an ancient and pre-scientific worldview but the truth is this belief persists even in our materialistic age. For example, many mainstream, non-Christian movies portray evil spirits as powerful and destructive supernatural forces. Minds that can be extremely sceptical under other circumstances seem very willing to suspend disbelief while in the movie theatre.

It seems that even our supposedly secular society cannot completely let go of a supernatural worldview – especially a belief in angels and demons.

And it is right not to because unholy spirits do exist, just as angels most assuredly do.

Worse still, these unclean spirits obey the bidding of an organizing, malevolent intelligence known as Satan, and Satan presents himself not as a dark and sinister angel but as an 'angel of light' (2 Corinthians 11:14). In other words, he deceives people – including Christians – by appearing enlightened not by appearing devious.

That being the case, we should not be too hasty to approve prophetic words, even ones which contain insights that look supernatural. Just because something *seems* truthful doesn't mean that it is *true*. If it was obviously false it would succeed in deceiving no one. Deception so often works because it is darkness masquerading as light; it is error disguised as truth. We therefore urgently need the gift of discernment, especially in our current age where there are many people with psychic and occult abilities that sometimes look similar to the gift of prophecy.

Discernment is the antidote to the toxin of deception.

Have you ever been deceived by the enemy into thinking that something false and destructive was in fact true and godly?

....

....

....

....

....

....

How then do we tell truth from error, light from darkness, when it comes to prophetic words?

Let me begin by saying two things.

Firstly, don't abdicate your responsibility to someone else in the body of Christ. Some believers tend to think like orphans rather than sons and daughters here. They leave it to others to decide what is true and what is false rather than exercising their own responsibility.

My view is that every believer needs to learn to weigh prophetic words. When Paul says in 1 Corinthians 14:29 that two or three prophets should speak in a meeting, and that 'the others' should weigh carefully what is said, 'the others' refers not to a group of prophets but to every believer present.

Let's accordingly think like sons and daughters in this matter. Let's all learn to discern. Let's deepen our knowledge of the Bible and our love of the Holy Spirit so that we will be able to expose any deception in our own lives and in the lives of other people in the body of Christ.

Secondly, we must take our time in discerning what is true and what is false, what is motivated by the Holy Spirit and what is not.

If you look at the ministry of the Apostle Paul you'll see that sometimes he knew very quickly that someone was being inspired by an evil spirit.

For example, when Paul was preaching the gospel to a Roman proconsul in Cyprus, a Jewish sorcerer known as Elymas tried to turn the proconsul away from the Christian faith. Paul knew instantly that this man was motivated by an unholy spirit. He rounded on him and said:

'You are a child of the devil and an enemy of everything that is right! You are full of all kinds of deceit and trickery. Will you never stop perverting the right ways of the Lord? Now the hand of the Lord is against you. You are going to be blind for a time, not even able to see the light of the sun.'

(Acts 13:10–11)

On other occasions, Paul took much longer in discerning if a person was telling the truth or not, whether they were inspired by the Holy Spirit or deceived by unholy or lying spirits.

So, in Acts 16, when Paul and his away team were proclaiming God's Word in the city of Philippi, they were followed wherever they went by a fortune-teller who shouted out to everyone that they were servants of the Most High God and that they were telling people how to be saved.

On the surface of it this sounds like truth-telling. Indeed there is nothing false in what this woman said. In fact, she was well known in the city so her commendation was on the surface of things extremely beneficial to Paul.

Yet, after many days of this Paul became annoyed and told the spirit that was influencing this woman to leave her. The spirit left her immediately, leaving the woman stripped of her occult ability (and indeed a very lucrative source of income from it).

Paul accordingly took his time in this instance.

So we all need to learn to discern.

Sometimes this discernment involves a gradual evaluation not just a sudden revelation.

Are there areas of your life right now where you need discernment to know whether God or the devil is behind it all?

....

....

....

....

....

If the gift of discernment is likened to the nose of the body of Christ then it would be fair to say that the church today needs to have its sense of smell restored.

The gift of discernment has been greatly neglected. It's time it was restored. It's time it was reactivated by all believers.

As Paul says to the church in Thessalonica:

> *Do not treat prophecies with contempt but test them all; hold on to what is good, reject every kind of evil.*
>
> (1 Thessalonians 5:20–22)

How then do we do exercise discernment? How do we learn to discern what is true from what is false, especially in relation to prophetic phenomena?

Here are a number of questions to ask whenever you are given prophetic revelation in any form:

1. Does this have a ring of truth?

This is by no means an infallible indicator but sometimes you will just know that something is true and authentic, or false and unreliable, when it comes to prophetic revelation.

Sometimes you will get what has been called 'a quiver in the liver' when you hear or receive a prophecy. In other words, you'll have an inner sense that this is something given by the Holy Spirit, that this is something that reveals the mind of Christ to an individual or to a church.

At other times you may get what some have described as 'a shiver in the liver'. In other words, your inner alarm system will go off and you'll think to yourself, 'I don't think that sounds like the Holy Spirit to me. This doesn't sound like the kind of thing Jesus would say or do.'

We shouldn't despise this more personal and subjective test when it comes to discerning what is from the Holy Spirit or not.

THE GIFT OF DISCERNMENT

In Acts 16:18 Paul discerned that the woman had an unclean spirit, not by subjecting her words to a list of objective criteria but by being attentive to what he felt in his spirit. Even though what she was saying sounded right and true, Paul had a shiver in his liver. Luke says in Acts 16:18 that he was 'annoyed'.

It may have taken a while for him to get in touch with these sanctified emotions, but once he did he moved from intuition to confrontation. So don't be afraid of your feelings. Sometimes the hunch that you're experiencing may be the Holy Spirit.

2. Does this look or sound biblical?

I have a friend who's fond of saying, 'The Holy Spirit does not speak with a forked tongue.'

Aside from the allusion to a snake here (an obvious symbol of deception), the forked tongue metaphor is a useful one.

The truth is that the same Holy Spirit who inspires genuine prophecy also inspired the Bible, the Word of God. It is therefore inconceivable that the Holy Spirit would say something through a prophetic word that cut across or contradicted what he said through the Scriptures.

Put another way, the Holy Spirit does not say something through a spoken word that in any way undermines what he has said through the written Word.

The Bible is our infallible guide for all matters relating to belief and behaviour.

Prophetic words, on the other hand, are fallible.

While the Bible stands forever, prophecies will pass away. The written Word is permanent and complete. Spoken, prophetic words are temporary and partial.

What this means is that every prophetic word, dream, vision or whatever needs to be judged and evaluated according to how consistent or inconsistent it is with what the Bible says. In fact, we would do well to learn from the noble Bereans in Acts 17:11. They listened to the words that Paul uttered and then examined the Scriptures every day to see if these things were true.

3. Does this sound like your loving Father?

Another question we should always ask is this: 'Does this sound like my loving, heavenly Father?'

God is the most kind and loving Father in the universe. The Bible in fact says that '*God is love*' (1 John 4:16). This means that our Father's thoughts towards us are affectionate and warm, noble and true, good and kind.

Some in recent years have tried to undermine this reassuring truth by claiming that it is God's righteousness not his love that the Bible emphasizes.

I don't in any way want to suggest that God's righteousness is not one of his primary characteristics, but to say that the Bible doesn't portray God as a loving Father is a dangerously mistaken view.

The most famous of all Jesus' parables is sometimes wrongly referred to as 'the parable of the prodigal son'. It is not really about the son at all but the most relentlessly compassionate and loving Dad you could ever read about. In fact, I doubt whether any storyteller in history has ever portrayed a father as lavishly loving as this.

Now a parable is a little story with a big idea. So what's the big idea here?

The big idea is that God is not some remote and volatile deity in the furthest heavens but that he's a forgiving, demonstrative, party-throwing Daddy.

The big idea is not that God is rich in anger and slow to love but that he is rich in love and slow to anger.

The father in the story is a revelation of the God and Father of our Lord Jesus Christ. And this is a loving Father.

Jesus said to his disciples, '*The Father himself loves you dearly*' (John 16:27, NLT). The words 'loves you dearly' are a translation of the Greek verb *philein* which has the connotation of demonstrated affection.

It is therefore utterly untrue to say that the New Testament doesn't present us with the revelation of the Father's love. Everything Jesus said and did was a window onto the Father's love (John 14:8–9).

And so I return to testing prophetic words and the question, 'Does this sound like my loving, heavenly Father?'

To answer such a question, we should become familiar with the intonations of the Father's voice. We are God's royally adopted sons and daughters. We are not religious slaves who don't know their Master's mind and who are ignorant of the tender tones of their Master's voice. We are princes and princesses in the kingdom of heaven who have a secure place close to the Father's heart and who have access to his thoughts and words, even his quietest whispers. And we know that his voice is a 'kind' voice. Even when the Father is displeased with us, his voice will be kind because it is the kindness of God that leads to repentance (Romans 2:4).

Whenever we receive prophetic revelation, either ourselves or from someone else, we should always ask, 'Does this sound like my heavenly Papa? Does it sound kind? Does it reveal more of his love?'

This is why the Apostle Paul emphasizes the importance of love in the exercise of the gift of prophecy. In 1 Corinthians 13:2, he says:

> *If I have the gift of prophecy and can fathom all mysteries and all knowledge, and if I have a faith that can move mountains, but do not have love, I am nothing.*

My advice is to ignore or reject any word that does not reflect the loving, fatherly heart of God.

If it is angry, aggressive, abusive, don't listen to it. Just because it is shouted, doesn't mean it is God. Volume is no indication of authenticity.

4. Do other Christians witness to it?

One of the most beautiful things about the church is that it is supposed to be a prophetic family. In other words, the church is a home in which every member of the family – whatever their age or background – is able to prophesy. This is the clear message of Acts 2:18–19 where Peter preaches that every believer from Pentecost onwards can now prophesy, even our sons and daughters.

If the church is meant to be a prophetic family, then we need to be interdependent not independent in our attitude towards prophecy. If I receive a prophecy from the Lord, I need to act as a responsible member of the family and ask others if they think it's from God.

In other words, I mustn't act like an orphan and be independent and rebellious. I must act like a daughter or a son and be relational and accountable. When it comes to prophetic revelation, we need to ask whether our adopted sisters and brothers witness to the truth of it.

If others in the family – especially older and wiser family members – sense that it might be from God, then we can hold fast to the word. If they don't, then we should let it fall to the ground.

So enlist the help of trusted others in the discernment process. Don't engage in UDI – a unilateral declaration of independence.

5. Do other prophecies confirm it?

There is a principle in Scripture, that the testimony of two or three witnesses confirms a matter (see Deuteronomy 17:6; 19:15; John 8:17; 2 Corinthians 13:1). This is a principle from the law courts and it essentially means that when two or three testimonies agree, then a matter is proven to be true. One witness alone is insufficient.

This principle can very helpfully be applied to the matter of prophecy. If two or three people who have the gift of prophecy give the same revelation to you, and there is no way they could have conferred with each other, then the word has a high level of credibility and authority.

6. Does it bear fruit?

In Matthew 7:20 Jesus says this about true and false prophets:

'By their fruit you will recognize them.'

One of the most important questions to ask of any prophecy is to do with consequence. What kind of result does it lead to?

In 1 Corinthians 14:3 Paul tells us that prophecy is given to comfort, encourage and strengthen the body of Christ, which is the church. We should therefore ask whether a prophetic word leads to the growth of the church both spiritually (in terms of a holier and closer walk with Jesus) and numerically (new people committing their lives to Jesus)?

In my view, if prophetic words foster an attitude of destructive criticism of the church then they should be quickly discarded. If on the other hand they lead to people having a new vision of what the church could be, leading to a fresh boldness in sharing the gospel, then they should be respected.

When Andrew Williams and I wrote *Breakout*, we told the story of how the Holy Spirit called us to recalibrate St Andrew's Chorleywood from a 'come-to-us' to a 'go-to-them' church. The church had historically not emphasized corporate mission or personal evangelism. Now we were being called by the Father to engage in a new season in which the Holy Spirit was calling us not only to focus on the *up* dimension (worship) and the *in* dimension (discipleship) but the *out* dimension (reaching the lost with the Father's love).

In doing this, Drew and I relied heavily on prophetic words that God gave to us individually and indeed through others. For such a great endeavour, however, these words had to be subjected to a rigorous process of evaluation. In other words, we had to learn to discern what was from God.

Looking back, Drew and I saw the outstanding fruit from these prophetic words. We saw thirty-two missional communities born, hundreds of people committing their lives to Jesus, many people saved and healed, the poor reached and a church of well over 1,500 members established.

The good fruit in mission confirmed the good roots of the revelation. Although we sometimes have to wait a while before seeing it, the fruit of a word is a really robust test of the root of the word. Good fruit suggests a good root – in other words, it points to the strong possibility that the Holy Spirit is the source.

7. Does this prophecy point people to Jesus?

When it comes to discernment, always remember 1 John 4:1–3:

Dear friends, do not believe every spirit, but test the spirits to see whether they are from God, because many false prophets have gone out into the world. This is how you can recognize the Spirit of God: every spirit that acknowledges that Jesus Christ has come in the flesh is from God, but every spirit that does not acknowledge Jesus is not from God.

We should always remember that the Holy Spirit points people to Jesus. The third person of the Trinity loves to exalt the second person. It is like he is forever saying, 'No, don't look at me. Look at him . . . look at Jesus. See how glorious he is!' How wonderful is the Holy Spirit!

The gift of prophecy is a gift of the Holy Spirit. If the Holy Spirit points people to Jesus, then a genuine prophecy will always draw people's hearts closer to Jesus. Never forget what it says in Revelation 19:10:

It is the Spirit of prophecy who bears testimony to Jesus.

Keep in mind the context of these words. They occur in the book of Revelation, a book that reveals, discloses and unveils the majesty of King Jesus.

When a prophetic word bears witness to the real Jesus – the Jesus of the New Testament who was born of the Virgin Mary, proclaimed and demonstrated the kingdom, died for our sins at Calvary, rose in a physical body from the dead, and ascended to the right hand of God – then we may confidently give it our fullest attention. If on the other hand it exalts the person giving the prophecy or it points to a counterfeit Jesus, then we should expose it for what it is – false rather than true prophecy.

We can discern true prophecy from false very quickly by subjecting it to the question, 'Does this glorify the real Jesus?' Genuine prophecy always does what the book of Revelation does – it causes a quantum leap in our vision of the greatness of Jesus.

What was the most recent prophecy you received (either yourself or from another)? In what ways do these seven questions help you to discern whether the word was authentic or not?

....

....

....

....

....

Perhaps the most challenging area where we need to exercise the gift of discernment is in relation to our calling. Whenever we are faced with times of transition in our lives, we have to test the words we receive both ourselves and from others. We have to be discerning because so much is at stake when we uproot and change direction. Transitions that are motivated by human rather than divine initiatives are always costly. We have a responsibility to ourselves and to others to make sure that we hear the Father's voice clearly and accurately.

A question that I'm often asked is this: 'How do you know for sure if God is calling you to into a new role, ministry or walk of life? What are the criteria you use for discerning a genuine call of God from something that's born of the flesh or even of a spirit of deception?'

Over the years I have had to walk many people through a process of testing a call of God, especially the call to ordained ministry. During these years the Holy Spirit gave me what I call the STARS test.

S – Scripture
T – Testimony
A – Advice
R – Revelation
S – Situation

Many people mistakenly look to the stars today (mainly through horoscopes and star charts) for both revelation about their future and guidance about their present. But the stars are not a healthy and reliable source of direction for our lives. It is theology not astrology that will chart our course. In other words, it is not the stars but the one who made the stars who guides our steps. This is where the STARS acrostic comes in.

If you are weighing up a call that involves transition and upheaval, then ask the following questions:

- What **Scriptures** has your heavenly Father used to speak to you about this new sense of calling?
- What is the **testimony** of your heart in this matter? Do you discern the inner witness of the Holy Spirit in this?
- What **advice** have you received from older and wiser Christian friends – especially from those that have the confidence to challenge you?
- What prophetic **revelation** do you have from the Lord about this? Have you had any visions, dreams, pictures, thoughts, messages, etc.?
- Are there clues in your current **situation** suggesting that transition is imminent and a vocation to something new is upon you?

If you can provide compelling answers to these questions then there is a strong chance your sense of calling is genuine.

Do you have a sense of the Father calling you into something new? If so, how do you know that you've heard the voice of God in this matter?

....

....

....

....

....

As I finish this chapter, I want to mention two more things.

The first is this: the gift of discernment can be used in all sorts of different contexts, not just in evaluating prophecy.

Although the Apostle Paul pairs together prophecy and discernment, the gift of distinguishing between spirits can be used in relation to supernatural phenomena generally, not just to prophecy.

There have been all sorts of extraordinary phenomena in recent years which some quarters of the church have been quick to attribute to the Holy Spirit, from gold dust to gold teeth.

It is our responsibility to subject anything that purports to be a manifestation of the Spirit to the questions I have provided here. We should not too quickly assume that every spiritual phenomenon is the result of the Holy Spirit.

Sometimes we may not get a definite answer to the question 'is this from God or not?' Where we are uncertain, we should admit that honestly and make sure we neither emphasize the phenomenon in question nor build a theology on it. In these situations it is prudent to say, 'We don't know for sure whether this is the Holy Spirit. Given our uncertainty, we are not going to focus on it.'

Where something supernatural is clearly evidence of the manifest presence of God, we should give thanks to God and glorify his Son.

The second thing I want to stress is this: when it comes to discerning false from true prophecy, it is really important to spend time getting used to what's genuine if you're going to recognize what's fake.

There are people today whose job is to spend hours and hours feeling genuine bank notes. After many days doing this they can quickly and conclusively tell the real from the counterfeit. When a counterfeit note is introduced into the system, they discern that it is a low-quality fake bank note because they have become intimately and indeed intensely familiar with the texture of the real.

It is really important that we have people gifted in discernment in the church today – people who are quickly able to tell whether something that looks like a manifestation of the Spirit is a natural imitation or even a demonic counterfeit. This takes time to develop because the imitation or counterfeit can be very close to the real.

What am I going to do as a result of what I've learned in this chapter?

....,......................

....

....

....

....

....

....

....

....

....

....

....

....

8

THE GIFT OF TONGUES

To another is given the gift of speaking in different kinds of tongues.

1 Corinthians 12:10

> The gift of tongues is the God-given ability to speak in a
> language which is given supernaturally rather than
> learned naturally.

I became a Christian in 1977 at the age of 16. For the first five years of my Christian life I heard a lot about the Word but not very much about the Spirit. Consequently, I developed a great love for the Bible (which I have never lost, nor do I want to) but I also had a real ignorance about the gift and indeed the gifts of the Holy Spirit.

Then, while I was studying for an English Literature degree at Cambridge University, I came across a Christian couple who were 'charismatic Christians'. I had heard this phrase bandied about by those who had taught me after my conversion and it was always mentioned derisively, dismissively, as if 'charismatic Christians' were 'of the devil's party'.

The only problem with this was that my two new friends had embraced the same 'sound doctrine' that I had been taught, except that they also believed that every Christian needed to be endowed with the gifts of the Spirit mentioned in 1 Corinthians 12:1–11. These spiritual gifts are called *charismata* in Greek, the word from which we get 'charismatic'.

As I got to know them I saw that they were genuine, Bible-believing Christians who in many ways were far more mature and godly than me and in addition seemed to have a much greater level of love, joy and peace in their lives. Furthermore, they had a very strong faith in God's power to speak today through prophecy and to heal through miracles.

Even more challenging, they not only told me that they spoke in tongues – I actually heard them. And I remember well how I felt when I did.

Having never heard anyone speak in tongues before, and having never heard anything but negative comments about those who did, I was in the first instance ambivalent. On the one hand I remember thinking, 'I have been taught to be suspicious of such people; I need to get as far away from them as I can, as quickly as possible!' On the other hand I also thought, 'This is beautiful and it really sounds like the language of heaven.'

After several more months of friendship, in which my eyes began to open to the fact that the gifts of the Spirit did not cease at the end of the New Testament era, I became intensely hungry for the gifts of the Holy Spirit.

I had the Word – in the sense that I revered and read the Bible – but I didn't really have the Spirit. Or, to put it more accurately, I had the Spirit – how else could I have repented of sin and believed in Jesus at my conversion? – but the Spirit didn't completely have me.

And so one night I asked my friends to pray for me.

They gently explained that they were going to follow the New Testament model and pray for me with the laying on of hands. That had never happened to me before but I nervously agreed.

As they did, they prayed that I would be filled to overflowing with the presence and power of the Holy Spirit.

I didn't sense any great lightning bolts after they prayed this but I did feel extraordinary peace.

Then they asked the Lord Jesus to give me the gift of tongues.

As they prayed, I sensed something begin to form in my mouth: phrases, strange phrases; phrases that I hadn't ever heard before but which seemed to have the same structure as any conventional language.

Then I opened my mouth and I began to utter things that I didn't understand. Just a few words came out at first, then more and more. I didn't know what I was saying because the words – they were definitely words – were not familiar to me.

More than thirty years later I am still speaking those phrases when I worship God, either privately on my own or publicly with other people.

That eventful night in Cambridge all those years ago transformed my devotional life. I received the gift of tongues and was thereafter enabled to praise and to pray at a whole new level. I am forever grateful to my heavenly Abba Father for putting me in the path of these dear friends and for giving me this very precious gift of tongues.

What's your story when it comes to the gift of tongues?

....

....

....

....

....

....

....

We come now to the final pair of gifts in Paul's list of the *charismata* – the charismatic gifts listed in 1 Corinthians 12:7–11 – to the gifts of tongues and interpretation.

This would be a good moment to look again at the passage:

Now to each one the manifestation of the Spirit is given for the common good. To one there is given through the Spirit a message of wisdom, to another a message of knowledge by means of the same Spirit, to another faith by the same Spirit, to another gifts of healing by that one Spirit, to another miraculous powers, to another prophecy, to another distinguishing between spirits, to another speaking in different kinds of tongues, and to still another the interpretation of tongues. All these are the work of one and the same Spirit, and he distributes them to each one, just as he determines.

Let's begin by looking at the source of the gift of tongues, which is the same source as the other eight gifts in Paul's list.

SOURCE

This is a supernatural gift that is given to us by the Holy Spirit. It is not a natural linguistic skill that can be coached or created. The Apostle Paul is quite clear here that the gift of speaking in different kinds of tongues is a gift of the one and the same Holy Spirit. It is the Holy Spirit who gives the gift of tongues to us, not people.

While Christian friends can pray for us with the laying on of hands, they cannot give us their gift, they cannot teach us to use their own spiritual language, nor can they compel us to create our own. The gift of speaking in different tongues is a supernatural anointing of the Spirit. It is as supernatural as the insights given in the word of knowledge or the transformations wrought by the gift of miraculous works.

This does not mean that we are ever 'out of control' when we use this particular gift because we have a choice whether to use or not to use it. But it does mean that the gift of tongues is not earned or manufactured – it is given by the Spirit of God.

NATURE

The phrase, 'speaking in different kinds of tongues', is made up of at least two words in the original language. The Apostle Paul uses the word *lalein* in Greek which means 'to speak'. He also uses the word *glossa* which means 'languages'.

When we mention this particular gift we are talking about the God-given and supernatural ability to speak in a language that we have not learned by human, conventional means. This is not the ability to speak languages other than your own which we cultivate over time through formal education. This is the sudden ability to speak unlearned languages which the Holy Spirit gives us.

DIVERSITY

There are essentially two forms of language that it is possible to be given by the Holy Spirit.

The first is called 'the language of the angels'. Remember here how Paul begins the chapter in 1 Corinthians 13 on love. He writes:

If I speak in the tongues of men or of angels, but do not have love, I am only a resounding gong or a clanging cymbal.

Notice how Paul refers to speaking in the tongues (or better still 'the languages') of men and of angels.

The angels speak their own language just as we do.

Paul says here that it is possible for him to speak not only the language of human beings but the language of angels.

One of the languages which it is possible to be given is therefore the language of the angels. This is sometimes referred to by the Greek word *angelolalia*. This comes from *angelos*, 'angel', and *lalein*, 'to speak'.

But then there is another form of language we can be supernaturally given.

Remember the outpouring of the Holy Spirit on the day of Pentecost? The writer of Acts 2 describes how the disciples of Jesus were suddenly filled with the Holy Spirit and began to speak in other languages as the Spirit enabled them.

There were people from many different nations within the sound of their voices. They had come to Jerusalem from all over the world to celebrate the Feast of Pentecost, one of the three main pilgrim festivals of the Lord.

As the disciples of Jesus were filled with the Holy Spirit, they were supernaturally empowered to speak in unlearned foreign languages, so that the pilgrims from all the nations could understand them in their own native tongue.

This was evidently a miracle because we read in Acts 2:6–8:

> When they heard this sound, a crowd came together in bewilderment, because each one heard their own language being spoken. Utterly amazed, they asked: 'Aren't all these who are speaking Galileans? Then how is it that each of us hears them in our native language?'

The Galilean followers of Jesus had not been taught these languages at school. They were given the ability to speak them by the Spirit.

This supernatural capacity to speak unlearned foreign languages is sometimes known as *xenolalia*, from *xenos*, 'foreign', and *lalein*, 'to speak'. This is indeed a miracle!

SPEAKING ANGELIC LANGUAGE	• Heavenly tongue
SPEAKING FOREIGN LANGUAGE	• Earthly tongue

CONTEXT

From 1 Corinthians 14 we can say that there are two main contexts for the gift of speaking in different kinds of languages.

a. Private

In the secret place, the child of God can use this gift in worship and intercession.

Sometimes your own human language is not sufficient for saying just how much God means to you or just how deeply you feel about an issue that you're contending for in prayer. On occasions like these, the Holy Spirit comes to our aid and we start praying with a language not our own.

This is the devotional language of the angels who gather around God's throne in the heavenly places. In other words, it is not *xenolalia* but *angelolalia*.

b. Public

The focus of 1 Corinthians 14 is mainly public worship. Paul's instructions about speaking in tongues are primarily directed to the gathered community. So it's not only the case that you can use this gift in private. You can also use it in public. In public worship you can join in with the angels in heaven and sing God's praises in a language not your own – something you can do with others who are able to sing in tongues.

You can also speak out in an unlearned foreign language if the Holy Spirit moves you to, enabling foreigners in the congregation to understand your worship in their own native tongue.

There are accordingly different contexts for using the gift of tongues. The more we learn to operate in this gift in the private place, the more we will be confident in using it in the public place.

DIRECTION

The Apostle Paul states that the language we speak under the anointing of the Holy Spirit has God as its focus. In other words, when a believer speaks in either angelic or unlearned foreign languages, he is speaking to God not to other believers or, for that matter, to unbelievers.

In 1 Corinthians 14:2 Paul explains that whenever we speak in tongues we speak to God not to people. If we speak in tongues in the private place, then we speak to God. If we speak in tongues in the public place, then we speak to God.

Tongues speech is the language of worship. This applies to the gift of tongues whether we are speaking the language of angels or the languages of other nations.

Even when the 120 disciples spoke in tongues on the day of Pentecost, their words were addressed to God. They praised God under the influence of the Spirit in unlearned foreign languages. Remember what the foreigners say to one another (Acts 2:9–11):

'Parthians, Medes and Elamites; residents of Mesopotamia, Judea and Cappadocia, Pontus and Asia, Phrygia and Pamphylia, Egypt and the parts of Libya near Cyrene; visitors from Rome (both Jews and converts to Judaism); Cretans and Arabs – we hear them declaring the wonders of God in our own tongues!'

They hear the earliest church declaring the wonders of God!

Even with *xenolalia* the language is devotional.

This is a really important point because whenever tongues are interpreted, the translation should normally be something God-directed. It should be a heartfelt statement of adoration from earth to heaven. It should not be a prophetic word from heaven to earth. The direction of tongues speech is towards the triune God – Father, Son and Holy Spirit.

DURABILITY

One of the claims made by some Christians is that the gift of speaking in different kinds of tongues died out with the New Testament era. In other words, some argue that the durability of this gift did not extend beyond the first century AD.

If we go to the Scriptures there is absolutely no biblical text which states or even implies that only Christians within New Testament times were supposed to receive and use this gift. In fact, the opposite is true. There is one passage that shows that believers will be speaking in tongues until the climax of history. I am referring to 1 Corinthians 13:8–10 where Paul says:

> *Where there are prophecies, they will cease; where there are tongues, they will be stilled; where there is knowledge, it will pass away. For we know in part and we prophesy in part, but when completeness comes, what is in part disappears.*

These words occur in a magnificent chapter on the subject of love. Paul says that true love lasts forever. He then contrasts this with three of the spiritual gifts – prophecy, tongues and knowledge. These will not last forever.

The key question then is, 'When will these gifts cease?' There is nothing to indicate that Paul thought they would cease when the New Testament era ended. Rather, Paul says they will cease 'when completeness comes'.

The word translated 'completeness' is a word which can also be translated 'the end'. What Paul has in mind here is the end of history, when Jesus Christ returns. When the end comes we won't need the gifts of prophecy and tongues any more.

Why will these gifts cease when Jesus comes back? They will cease because these gifts are 'partial'. They involve an incomplete knowledge of God's heart and ways. When the end comes, however, we will have a full knowledge of these things. When the end comes, there will literally be heaven on earth.

And in the new heavens and the new earth we will speak the language of heaven completely and fluently, not partially and falteringly.

LIMITATIONS

Some Christian movements and denominations have given the gift of tongues first place, and in the process have ignored what Paul says and implies about its limitations. We should note in particular the following:

- The gifts of tongues and interpretation occur at the very end of the catalogue of nine spiritual gifts in 1 Corinthians 12:7–11, so Paul purposely gives them lesser prominence not greater.
- The gift of tongues is last in the list of spiritual gifts that Paul lists in 1 Corinthians 12:28, after the gifts of 'helping and guiding' – a clear indication that he doesn't want people to give it first place.
- The gift of tongues has the capacity to turn unbelievers away from the church; indeed it may lead unbelievers to think of the church as a community of religious nutcases (1 Corinthians 14:23).
- The gift of tongues is incomprehensible without an interpretation (1 Corinthians 14:6) and is therefore of less value than prophecy, which is immediately intelligible.
- The gift of tongues is the only gift which requires another gift if it is to be fully edifying – namely the gift of the interpretation of tongues, without which the gift of tongues turns everyone into a 'foreigner' (1 Corinthians 14:11).
- The gift of tongues, exercised by many believers at the same time in a time of Christian worship, produces a cacophony of noise which does not honour God or provide clarity (1 Corinthians 14:7–9).

- The gift of tongues is a non-rational gift which leaves the mind unproductive; in that respect it is of less value than a gift like prophecy, which engages our thought processes (1 Corinthians 14:14–19).

How much emphasis do you yourself and the church you belong to give to the gift of tongues?

....

....

....

....

....

....

Having mentioned some of the limitations of the gift of speaking in tongues you might be forgiven for thinking that it's not a gift worth having. This is not at all what I want to imply. There are in fact many benefits to being given this gift. Let me mention just a few.

If using this gift is the same as speaking the language of the angels, then every time we speak in tongues either privately in the secret place or publicly in the worship place it releases more of heaven in our midst. The kingdom of heaven comes when we speak or sing in the language of angels.

Further, the gift of tongues is a great gift to use when you run out of words to express just how great God is. Sometimes human language isn't adequate for our praise. What an inspiring thing it is to be able to join in with the angels and use their language as we give voice to our heartfelt adoration of the Most High God.

In that respect, the use of tongues in thanksgiving and praise is an act of surrender. When we move from our own resources to the resources of the Holy Spirit, we relinquish control of our lives to the Lord. Every time we praise or pray in the Spirit, we say to God, 'I surrender all.'

We pray with our spirits rather than with our minds. Indeed, we rest our minds from their ceaseless activity.

It requires childlike humility to speak or sing in tongues. Remember that the gift of tongues is a form of communication in which you are expressing your feelings in a non-verbal, even pre-verbal way. This is what infants do. Infants cannot speak regular, conventional human language. This is why they are called 'infants' (from the Latin *infans*, meaning 'unable to speak'). So they express their feelings through wordless sounds. When we come before our heavenly Father and convey how we feel about him in tongues, we are effectively positioning ourselves before him as little children, revelling in his divine love.

If using this gift means using the language of heaven, no wonder it brings with it such a sense of the presence of God. All the gifts of the Spirit are manifestations of the presence and this is markedly true of the use of tongues. Whenever a person or a group of people start to use this gift, we become aware that God is truly among us. It's as if the Father is irresistibly drawn to the sound of his children expressing their love for him with such holy desperation and abandonment. Here, as with all the gifts of the Spirit, unwrapping the *presents* reveals God's *presence*.

In summary: there are many blessings to using the gift of tongues.

- It brings a sense of heaven on earth, especially when the people of God sing together harmoniously in the Spirit.
- It releases us from our frail attempts to find human words for adoring the infinite God.
- It enables us to give our minds a rest and to move from relying on our resources to the resources of the Spirit.

- It takes us to a whole new level of surrender to God as we yield our spirits, souls and bodies to him.
- It helps us to become like little children before God, speaking to him in the non-verbal sounds and sighs of a child.
- It brings a tangible sense of the manifest presence of God into the private and the public place.

No wonder the Apostle Paul says that anyone who speaks in tongues edifies themselves. No wonder he says that he'd like every believer to speak in tongues (1 Corinthians 14:4–5).

What are the benefits of speaking in tongues in your own walk with Abba Father?

....

....

....

....

....

....

INTERCESSION

Up until now I have been talking about the gift of tongues as the language of wordless and enraptured praise. But the gift of tongues can also be used in intercessory prayer – in praying for other people, situations, nations, and so on.

In Romans chapter 8, the Apostle Paul talks about how the Holy Spirit empowers us when we are confronted by our weakness in prayer. In verses 26–27 he writes:

The Spirit helps us in our weakness. We do not know what we ought to pray for, but the Spirit himself intercedes for us through wordless groans. And he who searches our hearts knows the mind of the Spirit, because the Spirit intercedes for God's people in accordance with the will of God.

Notice the reference to 'weakness' here. 'Weakness' doesn't mean a lack of physical strength. It refers to the inadequacy of human language in intercessory prayer. Weakness means the stunning realization of the frailty and finitude of human vocabulary when praying with an unusual depth of feeling for the needs of others, especially for 'God's people' (to quote Paul here).

When our hearts are drawn out in compassion towards those in the body of Christ who are going through painful times of trial, we are confronted by our own inability to say in words what our hearts really feel. Our vocabulary falls well short of our empathy. It's as if we are moved 'beyond words'.

It is at this moment, Paul says, that the Holy Spirit intercedes within us. As that happens, 'wordless groans' begin to pour out of us. Internally, our hearts are inflamed by divine love and compassion as the Spirit of God prays in and through us. Externally, our mouths emit wordless groans – or sighs too deep for words.

As that happens, the Holy Spirit connects us to the intercessory prayer of the ascended Son before the Father in heaven (Romans 8:34). Through intercessory tongues speech, we join in with the high-priestly prayer of Jesus before the throne of God. We are invited into the unending flow of love between the three persons of the Trinity – a love expressed in perfect, perpetual prayer for the children of God and for the lost boys and girls of this estranged planet.

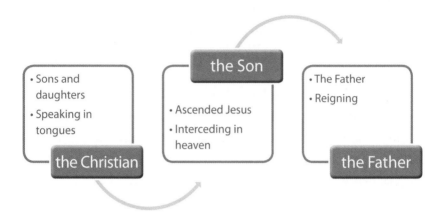

[The arrows here represent the Holy Spirit, who joins our prayers to
those of Jesus, and is the bond of love between the Son and the Father]

Truly, we need the gift of tongues in intercession. Whether in the
secret place on our own, or in a time of intercessory prayer with
other Christians, this gift is immensely valuable. It truly edifies us –
strengthens us – in our weakness.

Have you ever used the gift of tongues in intercessory prayer?

....
....
....
....
....
....
....

SINGING IN THE SPIRIT

Another area where the gift of tongues is invaluable is when we are singing to the Lord our songs of worship and thanksgiving. In 1 Corinthians 14:15, the Apostle Paul simply says, '*I will sing with my spirit*'. There are few sounds more beautiful than the sound of a congregation of passionate worshippers of God singing 'with their spirits' (that is, singing in tongues).

Singing in tongues involves going beyond the written words of our hymns and worship songs. Singing in tongues involves a breakout in spontaneous, Spirit-led adoration.

The first time I heard this was in the 1980s when I was asked to speak at a meeting of young people.

We met together in a large shed and there were about twenty present. As we all sang the songs on our song sheets, there came a moment when all of us felt led to depart from what had been prepared.

One person began by singing in tongues, lingering on a solitary note. Then others joined in, singing in cascading harmonies, until the whole group was singing in their own devotional languages.

The music came and went in undulations and crescendos.

I don't know how long it lasted but I do remember afterwards that all twenty of us felt as if there were hundreds, even thousands, singing. The angels had clearly joined us.

The room had become a thin place – a place where the gap between heaven and earth was so thin it was almost non-existent. We were not alone in that old and unremarkable shed. Heaven had invaded and I don't think any of us would be the same again.

When it's genuine, singing in tongues can be the most uplifting of experiences. It truly lifts you up.

But we also have to take great care here. Sometimes singing in tongues can lose its awe-evoking spontaneity and can become as predictable as written prayers.

I well remember seeing a Sunday evening service sheet in a charismatic church where I was preaching. There was a group of about five songs after my message. The fourth was 'We Exalt Thee'. After those words there was a line before the fifth song on which was written the letters PSH. Confused, I asked the man who was leading the service what PSH stood for.

'Oh, that means "Programmed Spontaneous Happening". We have learned that this song, 'We Exalt Thee', nearly always leads into singing in tongues. So those three letters are a signal to the worship team to be ready.'

What an astonishing contradiction in terms! When it comes to singing in the Spirit, the gift has to be used in a spontaneous not a planned way if it is to bring heaven to earth.

> **What experience have you had of singing in the Spirit, either privately or publicly?**
>
> ....
> ....
> ....
> ....
> ....

IS EVERY BELIEVER MEANT TO RECEIVE THE GIFT OF TONGUES?

This is a hotly debated issue and I have no intention or desire to introduce a note of controversy here. But there are a few simple truths we need to stress.

In the earliest church, many new converts received the gift of speaking in tongues when they were filled with the Holy Spirit. Take for example the first Gentiles to become Christians. As Peter preaches the gospel to Cornelius and his household, the Holy Spirit falls upon them all. Luke writes in Acts 10:44–46:

> *While Peter was still speaking these words, the Holy Spirit came on all who heard the message. The circumcised believers who had come with Peter were astonished that the gift of the Holy Spirit had been poured out even on Gentiles. For they heard them speaking in tongues and praising God.*

Some new believers clearly spoke in tongues when they first put their trust in Jesus Christ. But it isn't true to say that every new convert spoke in tongues, not according to the book of Acts. There are a number of references to people believing and being baptized in water but they don't all include descriptions of the new coverts speaking in tongues. For example, in Acts 18 Paul preaches the gospel to the members of the synagogue in the city of Corinth and Luke records:

> *Crispus, the synagogue leader, and his entire household believed in the Lord; and many of the Corinthians who heard Paul believed and were baptized.*

No mention of speaking in tongues here.

There are also occasions where new believers are said to have been baptized in the Holy Spirit, but Luke doesn't mention that they spoke in tongues as evidence of their conversion. For example, in Acts 8 Peter and John travel from Jerusalem to Samaria to pray for those who have heard Philip's gospel preaching and come to faith. Luke reports in verses 15–17:

> *When they arrived, they prayed for the new believers there that they might receive the Holy Spirit, because the Holy Spirit had not yet come on any of them; they had simply been baptized in the name of the Lord Jesus. Then*

Peter and John placed their hands on them, and they received the Holy
Spirit.

No mention of speaking in tongues here.

We therefore need to be careful not to make claims for this gift
that are not consistent with the experience of the earliest Christians.

Two things, however, should be noted.

Firstly, Paul clearly wanted everyone to speak in tongues because
he recognized that it was a gift that edified the believer in a very
personal way (1 Corinthians 14:5). As far as Paul was concerned,
every believer should ask for and receive the gift of tongues.

Secondly, Paul's own experience was that not every believer had
received the gift of speaking in tongues. That is why he says in 1
Corinthians 12:27–30:

Now you are the body of Christ, and each one of you is a part of it. And
God has placed in the church first of all apostles, second prophets, third
teachers, then miracles, then gifts of healing, of helping, of guidance, and
of different kinds of tongues. Are all apostles? Are all prophets? Are all
teachers? Do all work miracles? Do all have gifts of healing? Do all speak
in tongues? Do all interpret?

Within the body of Christ, the church, there is a diversity of gifts.
So Paul asks the question, '*Do all speak in tongues?*' This is clearly a
question expecting the answer, 'No'. Not everyone spoke in tongues
then and not everyone speaks in tongues now. So while Paul clearly
wanted everyone to have the gift of tongues (because it edifies us), his
experience was that not every believer does.

Does this mean that we shouldn't eagerly desire the gift of
tongues? No, we should come before Abba Father knowing that he
gives good gifts to those who ask him. Speaking in tongues is a good
gift. It enables us to express our love for the Father in joyful adoration

and to express our love for others in compassionate intercession. Who in their right minds wouldn't want a gift like that?

If you haven't already, do you want to receive the gift of tongues?

....

....

....

....

....

....

....

Finally, what is needed to receive this gift?

The answer is to position ourselves as a little child before our heavenly Father and ask for him to give us this gift. The Bible teaches that when we are filled with the Holy Spirit we are moved to cry out 'Abba, Father'.

In Romans 8:15 we are told:

> *The Spirit you received does not make you slaves, so that you live in fear again; rather, the Spirit you received brought about your adoption to sonship. And by him we cry, 'Abba, Father.'*

The Spirit that we receive when we put our faith in Christ is the Spirit of adoption. When the Spirit of adoption fills our lives we are baptized in love. To be baptized means to be immersed and drenched. Once the Spirit of adoption pours into the recesses of our spirits and souls we are filled with the Father's affectionate love. From this moment, the deepest cry of our hearts is, 'Abba, Father.'

Not long ago I returned from an Israeli home where the father (a Hebrew speaking Jewish man who has come to know Jesus as his Messiah) was constantly called 'Abba' by his little children.

When I asked him if Abba was a formal word, he looked appalled and declared, 'Abba means "Daddy". It isn't formal; it's intimate.' And he stressed again, 'It's intimate.'

As soon as a person is baptized in love, they cry 'Dad', 'Daddy', 'Papa' to the God who created the universe. As the Abba-cry pours out of us, we become hungry for more and more of the Father's love.

This hunger for the Father's presence begins to captivate us to a point where human desperation and divine visitation meet. For what Father would not stoop to satisfy their thirsty child?

As Jesus said in Matthew 7:7–11:

Ask and it will be given to you; seek and you will find; knock and the door will be opened to you. For everyone who asks receives; the one who seeks finds; and to the one who knocks, the door will be opened. Which of you, if your son asks for bread, will give him a stone? Or if he asks for a fish, will give him a snake? If you, then, though you are evil, know how to give good gifts to your children, how much more will your Father in heaven give good gifts to those who ask him!'

So ask and go on asking for the gift of tongues. Be hungry for this precious gift. It will take your devotional life to an entirely new and glorious level.

What am I going to do as a result of what I've learned in this chapter?

....

....

....

....

....

....

....

....

....

....

....

....

....

9

THE GIFT OF INTERPRETATION

To another is given the gift of the interpretation of tongues.

1 Corinthians 12:10

The gift of interpretation is the Spirit-inspired ability to translate a public declaration in tongues into the language of the worshipping congregation.

It happened during my time as the vicar of a church on the north edge of the city of Sheffield. I had called a half-night of prayer in the sanctuary of the Victorian church building in which I regularly led worship services. There were about twenty of us who braved the cold, wintery night and gathered by candlelight to praise and to pray in the pews.

At some point as we moved past midnight I sensed the Holy Spirit moving deep within my heart, stirring me to speak out. This in itself was not an unusual occurrence; I had often sensed that build-up of loving pressure that accompanies an invitation to pray. But what I'd never experienced before was such a profound urge to speak in tongues, at least not publicly.

By that time I had been a Christian for nearly twenty years. Since my time at university, when I had received the gift, I had spoken in tongues frequently on my own in prayer. But this was the first time – and as it turns out, the only time – I had ever given a public declaration in tongues.

So I resisted at first because I was understandably nervous. But then eventually I surrendered. Compelled by love, the language started to pour out of me during a time of waiting on the Lord. It didn't last long, maybe twenty seconds at the most, but it echoed resonantly through the dark and dusty building. I knew in my spirit that this was the language of the angels. And I knew that I had just given the Father my deepest praise. But what I didn't know was what I had said.

In fact, I had never known the meaning of the words that I had uttered in tongues in my alone times with the Father. For two decades I had wondered what it was that I was saying. What did it all mean, in my own language?

Then a lady began to offer a translation of what I had said. It was not profound theologically. It was in fact very childlike and simple. It went like this: 'You are my Father. You pour out your blessings upon me like silver rain and I love you. I love you with all of my heart, my dearest Papa.'

That may not seem much to you but it meant everything to me. And it transformed the atmosphere in that old Gothic church. We all rose to our feet and began to sing and shout our adoration to Abba, Father in heaven. Our hearts had been ignited. Even the candles seemed to burn more brightly.

Have you ever heard an interpretation of a public utterance of tongues?

....

....

....

....

....

....

In this final chapter we come to the gift of interpreting tongues. I define this gift as 'the Spirit-inspired ability to translate a public declaration in tongues into the language of the worshipping congregation'.

Now I want to be clear from the start what kind of language this gift is designed to interpret or translate. Remember in the last chapter I identified the two kinds of languages that are spoken when someone exercises the gift of speaking in tongues.

There is first of all the kind that we see on the day of Pentecost in Acts 2. When the Holy Spirit fills the disciples they start declaring the wonders of God in foreign languages that they have never learned. This kind of tongues-speaking is called *xenolalia*, which means speaking in a foreign language.

The 120 disciples were Jewish followers of Jesus and their native language was Aramaic. Most likely they could also speak a popular, marketplace form of Greek and understand smatterings of Hebrew and Latin. But when the Spirit of God filled them they were able to praise God in languages that they had never spoken before, and the audience of international pilgrims in Jerusalem understood what they were saying in their mother tongue.

That truly was a miracle!

The second kind of language someone speaks when they are using the gift of tongues is the language of the angels. Through the power of the Holy Spirit, some of heaven's realities become our realities. We are able to speak – at least in part – some of the phrases and sentences that are spoken by the angels as they worship in the purest adoration before the throne of God in the heavenly realms. This kind of language is called *angelolalia* – speaking in an angelic language.

| SPEAKING ANGELIC LANGUAGE | • Heavenly tongue |
| SPEAKING FOREIGN LANGUAGE | • Earthly tongue |

When it comes to the gift of interpretation, we should note that interpretation is not required when it comes to *xenolalia*. When someone speaks miraculously in an unlearned foreign language, there is no need for a translation. The foreigner who is present immediately understands the statement.

On the other hand, if someone utters an angelic language in a public worship meeting, this most definitely requires translation. In fact, the Apostle Paul is adamant in 1 Corinthians 14 that whenever someone publicly speaks in tongues, it must be interpreted. Tongue speaking in public is just a set of meaningless sounds if there's no translation. Paul says in verses 7–8:

> *Even in the case of lifeless things that make sounds, such as the pipe or harp, how will anyone know what tune is being played unless there is a distinction in the notes? Again, if the trumpet does not sound a clear call, who will get ready for battle? So it is with you. Unless you speak intelligible words with your tongue, how will anyone know what you are saying? You will just be speaking into the air.*

Here Paul uses two telling metaphors to describe what it is like when believers speak in tongues but without any orderly interpretation.

In the first, he likens this to a music group of pipe players or harpists who produce a cacophony in which the melody cannot be discerned.

In the second, he likens it to a bugler whose sounds are so random that no one knows what it is he's calling them to.

In light of this, Paul stipulates that anyone who speaks in tongues publicly (and Paul has *angelolalia* in mind here), they should pray for an interpretation. Paul's reasoning is impeccable in verses 16–17:

Otherwise when you are praising God in the Spirit, how can someone else, who is now put in the position of an enquirer, say 'Amen' to your thanksgiving, since they do not know what you are saying? You are giving thanks well enough, but no one else is edified.

What value have you placed on the gift of interpreting tongues up until now?

....

....

....

....

....

....

The gift of interpreting a public utterance in tongues is a much-needed gift.

The truth is, however, it has been as neglected as the gift of discernment. There are two main reasons for this.

The first is because it occurs right at the end of Paul's list of gifts and at least in some people's minds it falls off the end.

Here is Paul's catalogue of gifts in 1 Corinthians 12 once again:

- The word of wisdom
- The word of knowledge
- The gift of faith
- Healing gifts
- Miraculous works
- Prophecy
- Discernment
- Speaking in different kinds of tongues
- The interpretation of tongues

Notice how the last of these gifts almost feels like a postscript.

A second reason why this gift can be underrated by believers is because it's the only one in Paul's list that requires another one of the gifts if it's to operate at all.

The gift of interpretation can only function where another gift – the gift of speaking in different kinds of tongues – is functioning too. This cannot be said of any of the other gifts. All the other gifts can stand alone and function on their own. Not so the gift of interpretation because this gift involves interpreting tongues. Specifically, it is 'the Spirit-inspired ability to translate a public declaration in an angelic tongue into the language of the worshipping congregation'. No one can use the gift of interpretation if there isn't first an utterance in tongues. In that respect the gift can so often be marginalized.

For the Apostle Paul, however, the gift was very important. When he gave guidelines on orderly, Spirit-filled worship in 1 Corinthians 14, he said this in verses 27–28:

> If anyone speaks in a tongue, two – or at the most three – should speak, one at a time, and someone must interpret. If there is no interpreter, the speaker should keep quiet in the church and speak to himself and to God.

Paul would not countenance a public tongue without an interpretation. This is because Paul is adamant that charismatic worship in the church should not descend into the chaos that characterizes pagan or occult frenzies.

Paul never wanted there to be chaotic, ecstatic shouting in church meetings. He longed for the gifts of the Spirit to be welcomed but he equally strongly longed for them to be stewarded responsibly. The gift of interpretation is accordingly invaluable in the church, not least for maintaining order within charismatic worship.

Why is it important to interpret a public utterance in tongues?

....

....

....

....

....

....

....

The gift of interpretation is more than just a practical gift. It is also a beautiful gift. It is a beautiful gift because it points to our interdependence as believers. When someone interprets a public tongue, this illustrates very quickly the way in which all the different body parts in the church are of equal value. It also highlights in an effective way how each different part of the body needs other parts to work properly.

We shouldn't forget that Paul's introduction to the gifts of the Spirit occurs within the same chapter in which he talks about the church as a body. In 1 Corinthians 12:21–23, Paul says this about the interconnectedness and interdependence of every member of the church:

> *The eye cannot say to the hand, 'I don't need you!' And the head cannot say to the feet, 'I don't need you!' On the contrary, those parts of the body that seem to be weaker are indispensable, and the parts that we think are less honourable we treat with special honour.*

This goes for the gift of interpretation. No one should minimize it. All should honour it. The gift of interpreting public tongues is a beautiful gift because it reminds us of the interdependence and equality of every part of the body of Christ. And it is a beautiful gift because it acts as a very vivid reminder of the church's experience of 'the fellowship of the Holy Spirit'.

When one person speaks publicly in tongues and another person accurately translates it, then this underlines the fact that believers live in a community of people connected, united and empowered by the cohesive love of the Holy Spirit.

Only the Holy Spirit – the third person of the Trinity – could give one person a tongue and another person the interpretation. When gifts like these are used in an anointed and authentic way, it confirms that the church is no ordinary assembly of people. It proves that the church is a community of people which experiences and enjoys the presence of God.

This presence is made manifest when the gifts of the Spirit are truly at work – when gifts like tongues and interpretation are in evidence. And when the gifts are operating responsibly and powerfully, believers are reminded that they are not a social club but a supernatural community. Of all the communities and tribes on the earth, the church alone is given the unique privilege of having the fellowship of the Holy Spirit.

It is the presence of God which is the unique and primary indication that we are the people of God. This is why Paul constantly emphasizes the importance of the Spirit. In 1 Corinthians 12:4 he says:

There are different kinds of gifts, but the same Spirit distributes them.

In 1 Corinthians 12:12–13 he says:

Just as a body, though one, has many parts, but all its many parts form one body, so it is with Christ. For we were all baptized by one Spirit so as to form one body – whether Jews or Gentiles, slave or free – and we were all given the one Spirit to drink.

It is the presence of the Holy Spirit that distinguishes the church from all other groups on the planet.

When one person speaks in tongues and another interprets, this is an impressive reminder that we are a people of the divine presence.

Have you ever thought of the gift of interpretation as a 'beautiful' gift?

....

....

....

....

....

....

How then does a person use this gift?

The person who has the anointing to translate a public utterance in an angelic language will usually go through a number of defining moments every time someone speaks in tongues in church.

EVALUATION

The first moment will be a moment of evaluation.

We should remember that speaking in tongues is not restricted to churches where the gifts of the Spirit operate. There are, broadly speaking, three types of non-Charismatic tongues (that is, tongues not inspired by the Holy Spirit) that we may come across.

1. Dramatic

The dramatic use of tongues occurs in drama, either on the stage or in movies. It is almost always associated with comedy.

One of the funniest examples is Jim Carrey in the film *Bruce Almighty*, who compels the actor Steve Carell to speak in tongues while reading the news live on air. Dramatic tongue speaking has been a time-honoured feature of comedy.

2. Demonic

One of the reasons why Paul wrote about the spiritual gifts in 1 Corinthians 12 was because he wanted the believers in Corinth to be aware of the wide gulf between their present charismatic experience and their previous pagan experience. At the beginning of 1 Corinthians 12 he reminds them that when they had been pagans they had been 'influenced and led astray to dumb idols' (v.2).

The words 'influenced' and 'led astray' imply an uncontrolled abandonment to spiritual ecstasy. This kind of experience was not uncommon in the ancient world. At the Oracle at Delphi, the priestess of Apollo would fall into a state of frenzy and then speak out unintelligible words. These words were then translated into Greek and given as an oracle to the one who had sought the will of the pagan gods.

This practice of ecstatic speech, usually manifested in trance-like states, was said to have been inspired 'by the spirit of a python'. This is the same spirit that Paul casts out of a woman in Philippi (Acts 16:16–18). It was – and is – a demonic counterfeit of the spiritual gift of speaking in tongues.

3. Drug-induced

People affected by drugs, neurological damage or psychotic disorders, can speak in sounds that resemble unknown languages.

Pagan ecstasy was often induced by drugs and intoxicants in the New Testament era, as it is today.

Psychoactive drugs such as opium, LSD, psilocybin and mescaline can cause people to speak in a foreign or made-up language or revert to the pre-verbal sounds they made in their childhood.

So the first key moment for the interpreter of a tongue involves evaluation. The one gifted in interpretation will recognize very quickly whether this tongue is dramatic, demonic, drug-induced or divine.

TRANSLATION

If the source is divine then a second key moment will involve translation.

The nature of the interpretation can vary. Some may just understand the general sense of an utterance. Others may receive a word-for-word translation. When a person is led by the Holy Spirit to interpret a tongue, there is accordingly a spectrum from general paraphrase to literal translation.

At this point I want to be clear about what Paul expected when a tongue was translated. He did not expect to hear a statement in which God speaks to us. That is prophecy. Rather, he expected to hear a statement in which someone speaks to God.

Paul makes this clear in 1 Corinthians 14:2 when he says that the person who speaks in tongues utters mysteries to God in his spirit.

In other words, he declares the secret passion of his heart to God.

When a person speaks in tongues, the interpretation should accordingly be *earth-to-heaven* rather than *heaven-to-earth*. It should not be a prophecy. It should be a statement of worship.

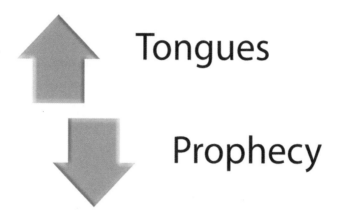

So in the second key moment in the process, the person gifted in interpretation will receive a Spirit-inspired translation of an utterance in tongues. That translation should be adoration not revelation.

DECLARATION

A third key moment involves the actual declaration of the interpretation of a message in tongues.

When a tongue is delivered in corporate worship, the 'interpreter' first evaluates whether this tongue is from the Holy Spirit or not. Then second, the interpreter is inspired by the Holy Spirit to understand the mysteries uttered in this heavenly tongue. This translation can be either literal or general. If it is general, then the chances are the interpretation that is offered may be shorter than the original utterance in tongues. If it is literal, then it may be slightly longer. Then third, the interpreter is empowered by the Holy Spirit to render a faithful translation of the utterance to the congregation. He or she steps out in faith and utters the earth-to-heaven sentiments expressed in the tongues speech.

Now I want to be clear what I mean here by a 'faithful' translation. A faithful translation is not just a translation which is faithful to the *content* of the utterance in tongues. A faithful translation is also a translation which is faithful to the *tone* of the utterance.

I have frequently been given translators or interpreters when I've delivered addresses in foreign countries over many years. The best of these 'interrupters' (as they are sometimes affectionately known!) not only give an accurate rendition of the sense of what I'm saying, they also feel the tone of what I've said and relay that as well.

When a person translates an utterance in tongues, they will have the same capacity to be sensitive to the tone of the original statement and will be capable of conveying that too, whether the tone is one of rejoicing or lamenting.

When an interpretation is faithful to both the content and the tone, then it will be greeted by a collective 'Amen'.

So the three main moments in the exercise of the gift of interpretation are:

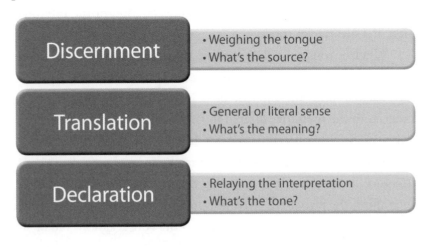

Discernment	• Weighing the tongue • What's the source?
Translation	• General or literal sense • What's the meaning?
Declaration	• Relaying the interpretation • What's the tone?

In what ways has this chapter changed your perspective on the gift of interpreting tongues?

....

....

....

....

....

....

In conclusion, all the gifts of the Spirit are valuable for the church. They are priceless presents from a very generous heavenly Father.

We should not marginalize the gift of interpreting tongues. The church needs interpreters. It needs people who are supernaturally endowed with a special ability to translate public utterances in tongues into the language of the congregation. When someone does this, it is a miraculous phenomenon. It reminds us that our heavenly Father is present, it increases our awareness of his power among us and it edifies the body because it takes us further up and further into the worship that is forever being offered up to God in the heavenly places.

Interpretation may be the last in the list of gifts. But it is not the least.

What am I going to do as a result of what I've learned in this chapter?

....

....

....

....

....

....

....

....

....

....

....

....

CONCLUSION

In this short study guide I've tried to impress on you the life-enriching truth that we all have a Father who has unique gifts to give each one of us – gifts which are designed to help us seize and fulfil our destiny here on the earth. He has presents for us which serve to confirm his presence.

If you're reading this and you are not a Christian, I'd like to encourage you to make a choice to put your trust in Jesus Christ, God's Son, to turn from self-love to the Father's love, and receive the gift of the Holy Spirit.

When you do, you don't just receive the gift of the Spirit, you receive gifts of the Spirit too.

You may start to speak in unlearned languages.

You may start to hear the Father speaking to you through dreams.

You may start to see sick people healed when you pray for them.

You may start to bring great clarity to complex issues through wise words.

You may start to see miracles.

Receiving the gift of the Holy Spirit is the portal, the gateway to operating in supernatural gifts that come from a perfect, loving heavenly Father.

If you are already a Christian, I'd like to urge you to grow in your hunger for the gifts of the Holy Spirit.

We are not supposed to be ignorant about the gifts.

We are certainly not to be dismissive of them.

We are called in the Bible to welcome the gifts of the Spirit in our lives and to use them faithfully and frequently for the benefit of others.

It is my prayer that this book will help you to discover what your gifts are and that it will incite in you a desire for more.

Remember what I said earlier in this book: the spiritual gifts are for the passionate not the passive. This means that the level of our anointing will be directly related to the acuteness of our hunger.

I want to add one final point. The nine gifts that I unwrap in this book are not the only gifts mentioned in the Bible. These have received most attention, particularly after the birth of the Pentecostal movement in the first decade of the twentieth century and the birth of the Charismatic movement in the 1960s. Pentecostal and Charismatic Christians have commonly tended to focus on the list of the gifts in 1 Corinthians 12:1–11. But there are other passages in the New Testament which mention gifts of the Spirit – for example, Romans 12:3–8:

> *For by the grace given me I say to every one of you: do not think of yourself more highly than you ought, but rather think of yourself with sober judgement, in accordance with the faith God has distributed to each of you. For just as each of us has one body with many members, and these members do not all have the same function, so in Christ we, though many, form one body, and each member belongs to all the others. We have different gifts, according to the grace given to each of us. If your gift is prophesying, then prophesy in accordance with your faith; if it is serving, then serve; if it is teaching, then teach; if it is to encourage, then give encouragement; if it is giving, then give generously; if it is to lead, do it diligently; if it is to show mercy, do it cheerfully.*

In this list Paul mentions a gift that we find in 1 Corinthians 12 (prophecy) but he also includes gifts that aren't:

- The gift of serving others
- The gift of teaching
- The gift of encouraging others
- The gift of leadership
- The gift of mercy

Don't ignore these gifts.

You may have a special God-given ability to serve other people in practical, Christ-like ways. That is a hugely important gift in the church. Those who have the anointing to serve are a priceless group within the Body. They are not the wishbones of the church, who spend all their time wishing that jobs were done while doing nothing themselves. Nor are they the jawbones, those who forever talk about doing things but who never get off their backsides to do anything. No, those anointed with the gift of service are the *backbones* of the churches worldwide. Without them, the whole community would collapse like a body devoid of a skeleton. If you have the gift of serving others, I praise God for you.

Then there's the gift of teaching.

If you have this gift, use it. There are not enough people who have the anointing for making old truths fresh and new. So many who enter the pulpit do not have the God-given grace to take a passage of Scripture and make it luminous and revelatory in the hearts and minds of their listeners. This is such a rare gift and the churches worldwide need to train anointed teachers as intentionally as they train prophets. If the church is to mature in the way that Paul envisaged when he wrote Ephesians 4, then it needs people with a powerful anointing to bring together a marriage of the Word and the Spirit and to help believers to feel as if the hour of the message brings the message of the hour.

Then there's the gift of encouraging others.

If you have the special, God-given ability to encourage other people through anointed texts, emails, cards, letters and gifts, then please don't see this as a second-class anointing. It is every bit as valuable as the supernatural ability to heal the sick.

I have a special file on my computer marked 'encouragements'. Here's the most recent:

> I don't know if you'll ever get this email but I wanted to let you know how much of an impact your book *From Orphans to Heirs* continues to make. For years now I have been preaching from it, teaching at conferences about it, and now I'm doing seminary work and using your book as an outline. The freeing nature of the message of *From Orphans to Heirs* has changed so many lives and has helped the non-believer find Christ and the scholar fall in love with God all over.

That dear brother in Christ didn't need to write this email. But he did. He took the trouble to find my address and to send this message and it warmed my heart.

Here's another message – my personal favourite:

> My wife and I are being enriched by your book *Every Day with the Father* which we read and pray every morning over breakfast. We are now on day 252.
>
> My wife went to the doctor back in June with a large 4.5cm hard lump on her leg. She was immediately referred for suspected cancer, and it isn't. A whole series of tests and scans and it has finally been diagnosed last week as either a ganglion or meniscal cyst – the doctor couldn't be sure which without operating. He said it wouldn't go away by itself and he could either operate or she could just keep an eye on it.
>
> On Sunday eve we were praying together for some time for something entirely unrelated, and afterwards I asked my wife to show me the cyst again. She did, it was still hard, the same size. Then she felt she should whack it with your book *Every Day with the Father* and

it immediately and completely disappeared, and there has been no sign of it since. Thought you may be encouraged that God is at work through your books, and in sometimes unexpected ways.

I was greatly surprised, delighted and fortified by that message!

If you have the gift of encouraging others, please use it. Your words might even be the difference between life and death for someone.

And if you have the gift of leadership, please use that too.

The church needs anointed leaders – people who have the God-given capacity to see the direction in which God wants to take his people and to encourage others in functional, relational and Christ-like ways to follow. True leadership is lacking in the world today but it is also lacking in the church. This is a time and a season in which the Father wants to give the anointing for pioneering, mission-shaped, adventurous leadership to people of trustworthy character. He wants to mobilize and energize people with an entrepreneurial and creative spirit to think outside the box and lead people into new apostolic expressions of church.

This is a time for the anointing of leadership.

It is also, finally, a season for the gift of mercy – that God-given ability to know the Father's heart for the poor and to bring freedom to those whose basic human rights have been robbed from them by oppressive social systems.

This is without doubt a season for God's dream for social justice to become a reality on the earth. The generation of 18–30-year-olds in the current church will not settle for any programme of mission or theology of revival which does not have justice at its epicentre. For the 'millennials' (as they are called), the social justice agenda in the mission of Jesus is right at the top of their priorities. As a result, the anointing for mercy rests very heavily and strongly upon them. They are a generation motivated by a compassion which simply has to find its expression through practical action. They are an army of reformers filled with the Father's love. They are angels of mercy on a merciless planet. They are world-changers and history-makers.

If you have the gift of mercy, find the Father's outlet for that and start bringing heaven to those who are experiencing hell on earth.

So there are other gifts besides those that I have expounded in the nine chapters of this book. Those gifts need to be understood and used as well.

But I want to finish by returning to the nine-fold gifts of 1 Corinthians 12 and share a meditation called 'I Believe'.

It is a heart's cry for the church to become truly charismatic again – in other words, filled with the presents which reveal the Father's presence.

This is a dream of a church in which every member has unwrapped their gifts and is using them to strengthen the church and heal the world.

I BELIEVE

I believe the church is a community of people who know the Father intimately, who love his Son Jesus Christ, and who live in the experiential reality of the Holy Spirit.

It is a community of adopted sons and daughters who honour the revelation the Holy Spirit brings and who communicate Abba's heart of love through the gift of prophecy.

It is a community of people whose worship of God is so alive in the Spirit that at times the children of God break from using human language to the language of the angels in heaven.

It is a community where public utterances in tongues are translated into everyday language, taking adoration of the Triune God to an even higher level than ever before.

It is a community in which gifted teachers bring the Bible to life under the anointing of the Spirit and where heavenly wisdom and knowledge is constantly imparted to God's people.

It is a community where surges of extraordinary faith are commonly felt and invasions of heaven frequently occur in extraordinary and awe-inspiring ways.

It is a community where the sick are supernaturally healed of every kind of physical and emotional affliction and where miracles happen, bringing glory to the Father.

It is a community where discernment is endorsed and exercised, and where only authentic and biblically sanctioned supernatural phenomena are welcomed.

It is a community where the practical gifts are valued as highly as the power gifts and where every part of the Body, however diverse, is equally esteemed.

It is a community in which people serve one another in often hidden ways, helping and encouraging others and revealing the Father's love and concern for individuals in the process.

It is finally a family where God's children constantly exercise mercy rather than judgement and where there is a furious passion to bring the Father's justice to the poor.

Put like that, the church sounds profoundly attractive doesn't it? Adorned with the gifts, the Bride of Christ looks bejewelled – dazzlingly beautiful.

We cannot do without the gifts of the Spirit. We must welcome them. We must eagerly desire them. We must exercise them.

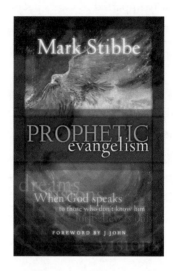

978-1-86024-457-5

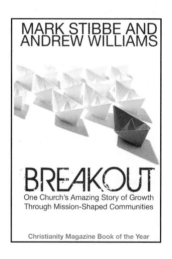

978-1-86024-596-1

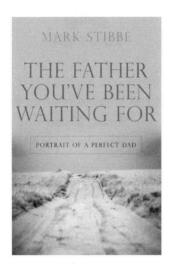

978-1-86024-593-0

978-1-86024-810-8

Authentic

We trust you enjoyed reading this book
from Authentic Media. If you would like to be
informed of any new titles from Mark Stibbe and
other exciting releases you can sign up
to the Authentic newsletter online:

authenticmedia.co.uk

Contact us:

By Post:
Authentic Media
52 Presley Way
Crownhill
Milton Keynes
MK8 0ES

E-mail:
info@authenticmedia.co.uk

Follow us: